THE IDEA OF PSYCHOLOGY

THE IDEA OF PSYCHOLOGY

Reclaiming the Discipline's Identity

Donald Lindskoog

HOWARD UNIVERSITY PRESS
Washington, D.C.
1998

Howard University Press, Washington, D.C., 20017

Copyright © 1995 by Donald Lindskoog

Manufactured in the United States of America

This book is printed on acid-free paper.

10 9 8 7 6 5 4 3 2 1

Library of Congress Cataloging-in-Publication Data

Lindskoog, Donald, 1937–
    The idea of psychology : reclaiming the discipline's identity / Donald Lindskoog.
      p. cm.
    Includes bibliographical references and index.
    ISBN 0-88258-200-3 (pkb. : alk. paper)
    1. Psychology—Philosophy.   I. Title.
BF38.L57   1998
150'.1—dc21
                                      98-15118
                                        CIP

For Verna
a meet help

Table of Contents

Preface

For some time, I have felt that the discipline of psychology is in an identity search not unlike that engaged in by some young adults. At 115 years of age, it has not yet clearly defined itself; it has not yet delineated the borders of its domain. Like a healthy young person, it has during its formative period tried on a number of different identities in an effort to explore its options. Some of them have been sedate and rational, others radical and daring. It seems to me that the experiment has proceeded in the youthful joy of uninhibited exploration.

Somehow trusting deeply that its unique identity will eventually emerge, psychology has freely borrowed from several available models. It has mimicked religion at times, pretending to be the new church and the new priesthood—this time a secular one. Uninterested in that game, a segment has aped biology and medicine, enjoying the sense of authority and prestige accorded physical science in this century. It has tried on other roles as well, including those of sociology and social work. And at other times it has imitated education, humbling itself to the teacher's nurturant caring task, basking in the glow of altruistic concern for others.

But this exploratory role play, valuable as it may be, has come at some cost. Outsiders are not quite certain who we psychologists are because we ourselves don't know. In the popular mind there is no clear distinction between us and

some other professional groups. As individual psychologists we busy ourselves in the luxury of choosing which of psychology's masks we personally
reject and which we choose to wear. And outsiders, finding one of our
various personas to their liking, choose to call *that* psychology, then
identify with it, and thereafter regard themselves as insiders, conveniently
forgetting all the other masks psychology offers. But for those of us who
work in the field, especially for those who teach psychology, it is not so
easy to disregard as alien the less preferred facets of our discipline. They
irritatingly present themselves to us at every turn.

Psychologists are in danger of remaining in an identity morato-
rium—never really deciding who we are and who we are not—because of
the fear of losing some of our options. I believe it is time for psychology
to commit to an identity. This is difficult, in the same way it is hard for
a young person to exclude some identity options in favor of a single one.

Psychologist Joseph Rychlak has recently written that psychological
theorists should try to stay within one "grounding realm" (1993). He
suggests that realm should be based on what he calls the *Logos*—a Greek
term denoting "word" but connoting much more, and, specifically for our
purposes, what I will call in this book *mind*. He argues for the primacy
of *Logos*, that psychology should not think of itself as deriving from *Bios*
(the biological "substratum") nor from the more general *Phisikos* (the
physical realm). One reason is that these derivative identities make ours
a derivative discipline. In taking this position, Rychlak deliberately identifies himself with the Kantian, rather than Lockean, line of philosophy,
affirming the existence of *Logos* as earlier than and independent of *Bios*.

Rychlak and all of us who stand with him on this issue by no means
represent an innovation in psychology, nor even a minor theme, when the
entire history of the field is considered. At its birth, psychology simply
presupposed the existence of mind and unabashedly defined consciousness
as its primary focus of study. But as it searched for an identity that would
have broad appeal in an age idolizing natural science, it experimented
with ways to redefine mind as secondary, or even to reject mind altogether,
incorporating mechanistic and Lockean presuppositions into whole systems of understanding people. In this process, incredibly, it systematically
excluded agency, personhood, and even the then-remaining vestiges of
mind.

Like all identity experiments, it was no doubt developmentally important for us to see where this exploration would lead. But now we know that it leads to an identity diffusion. Haltingly, starting with the cognitive revolution, we are making our way back to what continues to be a solidly empirical discipline that remains centered on mind. It is my hope that this book will assist us in that restoration.

To accomplish this purpose, who should read this book? As a lifelong college professor, I seek to sway students majoring in psychology. In the undergraduate psychology curriculum, this would best occur in a senior year history of psychology course for which the book could become a supplementary text. Alternately, it also would serve well for a seminar in psychological philosophy or epistemology.

The book, however, is *not* intended primarily for undergraduate readership but for all, especially professional psychologists, who have an interest in the way psychology continues to develop at the threshold of the twenty-first century. Phenomenally rapid growth in the sheer number of doctoral-level psychologists during the past three decades has given psychology severe growing pains and challenging new options that must now be consolidated within a revised, more mature and settled identity.

Within this book I explore the underlying reasons for psychology's developmental delay and offer suggestions to reclaim the discipline's distinctive identity. It is my hope that this work will move us toward that more mature identity.

Acknowledgments

I have received much help on this project and I am deeply grateful. President James Bultman and Dean Robert Zwier of Northwestern College (Iowa) were instrumental in providing me with a six-month sabbatical during which most of the writing was done. The sabbatical was spent at Cambridge University, England, as a Visiting Scholar in the Experimental Psychology department. I thank Professor N.J. Macintosh, Cambridge department chairperson, and other members of the department for their unfailingly kind hospitality.

Dr. Donald Wacome read an entire early draft and offered important philosophical corrections and suggestions. Deborah Menning and Christine Cotting spent many hours in the revising process, and their help was invaluable in improving the readability of the text. And my wife, Dr. Verna DeJong, gave me much help on both the book's structure and content, and was patient and understanding with me throughout. To all of these I express my profound gratitude.

1

Psychology's Diffused Identity

*F*irst psychology lost its soul and then it lost its mind. This pithy remark of exceptional insight is attributed to Carl Jung. He was referring to what he considered the erosion of cohesiveness within psychology as a discipline because of a loss of focus. The potential of integrity for any major human enterprise implies that it be based on a single idea. The word *integrity*, related to the verb *to integrate*, means that disparate elements are linked through an important unifying principle. That integrity may be expressed as an idea. The more powerful the integrating idea, the greater the integrity.

In this book, I will try to show that psychology at its best, both as an academic discipline and as a tool of intervention, has a powerful single integrating idea. This idea, however, has been more or less continually in jeopardy of being eclipsed by ideas, presently to be examined, that are less central to psychology's core at the same time the idea itself has been deprecated. These secondary and often derivative ideas, all worthy and many playing a legitimate part in the psychological enterprise, have masqueraded at different times and places as the quintessential heart of the venture. I will try to show that when this has happened, psychology has become disquieted and its energies diffused, rendering it ineffectual to its main purpose.

Why has there been this failure to maintain focus? In a way, this is a curious—even humorous—lapse by practitioners of a discipline that purports to teach self-knowledge and deliberate goal achievement. Nonetheless, it is like the many failures by individual psychologists to live according to their own principles. The psychologist who thwarts communication flow with a spouse, who makes catastrophies of small reversals, or who overuses aversive conditioning when parenting similarly illustrates less than thoughtful choice-making. In each instance, some stronger motive overruled the knowledge of the psychologist.

The very notion that a given academic discipline could have developed historically in a different and perhaps better way may be a foreign concept to many readers. The pervasive pragmatism with which most of us approach our life and work disinclines us to go back and review how choices at crucial points in the past might have resulted in a different way of viewing and doing things. We are predisposed to consider such efforts as a waste of time because those choices are behind us and because it is our task to cope with things as they are now.

On the contrary, I affirm that such effort involves time well spent. It enables us to learn from our own history so that we are not doomed to repeat and perpetuate its errors. In fact, we may discover that a few critical mistakes psychology has made are so close to the core of its identity that their correction can set the discipline on a clearly more productive path for the future.

CAUSES OF PSYCHOLOGY'S DRIFT

There are at least three reasons why psychology has been derailed from time to time. The first reason is the burden it shares with all groups that face the social marginalization that accompanies maintaining one or more distinctive viewpoints. This discomfort reduces the emphasis on distinctives and emphasizes commonalities with others because it is always easier to stand together on common concerns, sacrificing distinctives, than to stand alone. Thus, religious groups typically move from their narrow sectarian creeds and practices to more ecumenical and broadly acceptable views; that is, they move from sectarian status to denominational status.

Psychology also finds it difficult to remain true to its core commitment in eras of persistent or increased ideological hostility. [1]

A second general reason psychology has tended to abandon what I contend is its essence relates to its phenomenal growth in membership and status over the past three decades. It is relatively easy for a small corps of academics and practitioners to remain loyal to a unifying concept. But as numbers increase, heterogeneous perspectives grow. Personal rewards for expressing diversity of viewpoint concerning the nature of psychology come in the form of public recognition for individuals who seem, by taking a divergent path, to throw fresh light on difficult problems, or who, appealing to a different motive, even offer psychologists new ways to increase monetary profit.

Finally, and related again to personal rewards, is the temptation to provide psychology that is easily understood and assimilated. Notwithstanding the fact that one of modern psychology's important nineteenth-century roots was the popular psychology of mind cure, it is nonetheless true that the public at large has yet to appreciate a single, unifying concept of the basic nature of psychology. And because psychology's core idea is properly more circumscribed than the entire available range of causes for human behavior, the public required many decades of education about it. In the meantime, psychologists who have strong personal needs to communicate directly with the general public often fall back into a plethora of plausible nonpsychological modes of explanation.

BASIC WAYS PSYCHOLOGY HAS ACCOMMODATED TO POPULAR IDEAS

Alternative modes of behavioral explanation typically have their origins in history prior to psychology's beginning. Although there are several others, the two most threatening modes are theological and/or medical. For example, to account for human behavior, especially an unusual behavior, religious or quasi-religious people might point to a spiritual cause such as a moral choice that changes the individual's relationship to the spiritual world. Among the general public, a behavior might be attributed to a medical/physical cause such as a brain tumor or genetic predisposition. The view that behavior could be understood *apart from* any reference to either of these spheres of discourse is seldom appreciated and somewhat difficult to comprehend in our current culture.

The most concrete evidence that the theological and medical modes of behavioral explanation take precedence over other modes can be found in the category of professionals consulted by people in emotional or psychological need. Vandenbos, Cummings, and DeLeon (1992) report that the Joint Commission on Mental Illness and Health in 1955 found that "one in four respondents indicated he or she had experienced some type of psychological or behavioral problem during his or her lifetime for which professional help would have been useful," although only one in seven had sought such help. Of the group seeking help, "42% consulted clergymen, 29% consulted general physicians, 18% consulted psychiatrists or psychologists, and 13% went to social agencies or marriage clinics." (p. 85) Without discrediting the contributions made by clergy or physicians, I contend that neither group is professionally mandated to construe human problems in a genuinely psychological mode. Moreover, those people who consulted psychiatrists or social agencies before 1955 might not have experienced a psychological approach to dealing with their problems. While the picture has changed substantially since 1955, considerable confusion about what constitutes psychological versus medical or pastoral treatment persists.

The notion that such accommodation results in nothing being lost from one sphere of discourse to another may be further fostered by a too-close professional alliance among psychologists, clergy/theologians, and medical professionals.[2] Since the turn of the twentieth century in America, ministers and theologians have increasingly used psychological terminology while altering its psychological meanings in important ways. Examples of this misuse will be explored later. Similarly, medical doctors cast psychological terms into a physicalist explanatory framework, suggesting that the psychological ideas are merely metaphors for a biological explanation.[3] This practice is sometimes termed reductionism—reducing the truths of one discipline to those of another, supposedly more basic, discipline. As indicated, this reduction may be to a theological or physical explanatory principle that is presumed to be more ultimate and more directly related to phenomenal reality.

THE CENTRAL IDEA OF PSYCHOLOGY

We are prepared now to consider the thesis of this book: that a consistent faithfulness to the core idea of psychology simply will not permit its theories, findings, concepts, or intervention methods to be reduced to some reputedly more basic framework of discourse such as theology, medicine, or others. We will examine the familiar suggestions of well-intentioned religionists who claim that all conclusions of research psychology can be found in elementary, and perhaps purer, form within one or more of the world's religions; we will then see how this assertion undermines psychology's strength and damages its potential for social contribution. By the same token, the occasional public statements by physicians and devotees of natural science technology that medicine will eventually develop sufficient knowledge of the nervous system to render psychology virtually redundant fail to recognize or accept the radical idea at the heart of psychology.

What is that idea? Put succinctly, it is that in the evolving empirical discipline of psychology, a truly original and unique explanatory language has developed to name and understand an aspect of human experience that has never been named or understood before.[4] That is, in the same sense that biology, physics, economics, and astronomy distilled an aspect of "reality" that was thereafter regarded as an independent sphere of discourse, psychology is now properly considered to be autonomous and independent of other human fields of knowledge. This may be asserted despite the *ultimate* interdependence of all human fields of knowledge.

Comparing psychology to other established academic disciplines raises the philosophical question about what could be called the actuality of their subject matters. This question about the correspondence of curricula to things in the real world is underscored by the changes seen in university curricula from century to century: Do scholars in different centuries study the same raw phenomena under different topics, or do they study different phenomena? Although a resolution of these philosophic questions cannot be attempted here, it is pertinent to my main point to briefly raise this issue and disclose my own position.

CRITICAL REALISM

In regard to the phenomena disciplines treat, the position I take may be broadly termed *critical realism*. Critical realism views the phenomena handled by a discipline like history, literature, or music as having, within certain limits, some objective reality.[5] In other words, a discipline along with its subcategories is not simply a semantic abstraction from experienced reality wherein somewhat arbitrary divisions are created and labels are assigned to the concepts of the field. Instead, it is in some measure a description of that which it truly discovers.

One corollary to the critical realism position is that, when a new category of human knowledge and research emerges over a reasonably long time period (e.g., the 100-plus years of psychology), the category reveals a new dimension of human reality. The relationship between the new field and the one from which it came is an important question—one that I will address several times in this book. For now, I will refer to that relationship as *emergentism*: The new discipline represents a new configuration of truths (laws, principles, theories) that cannot be derived from those found at the original level. However, this emergentism refers to newly discovered reality and is not merely socially constructed.

This is illustrated well by the ancient gradual differentiation of medicine from theology. In the Bible, instructions are given to the Levitical priests concerning the diagnosis and treatment of skin diseases. The functions of priest and physician were inseparable and performed by the same person:

> When a person has on the skin of his body a swelling or an eruption or a spot, and it turns into a leprous disease on the skin of his body, he shall be brought to Aaron the priest or to one of his sons the priests. The priest shall examine the disease on the skin of his body, and if the hair in the diseased area has turned white and the disease appears to be deeper than the skin of his body, it is a leprous disease; after the priest has examined him he shall pronounce him ceremonially unclean (Leviticus 13:2–3, NRSV).

Confinement of the affected person was required under the authority of the priest. The Levitical writer goes on to detail various procedures for diagnosing erupting sores, boils, burns, and diseases under head or facial hair. Toward the end of the chapter, he turns to leprous diseases that appear in clothing, "in warp or woof of linen or wool" (verse 48). This ascription of disease to nonliving as well as living entities—echoed elsewhere in Levitical law where walls of houses are said to be likewise infected—indicates an as yet undifferentiated concept of disease. To this point, a disease is more or less synonymous with some worrisome flaw.

Later, as living and nonliving entities were gradually differentiated, a distinction that came to be seen as crucial to effective diagnosis, the healer's task became conceptually more restricted and specialized. The priest's conceptual categories became inappropriate and less useful to the tasks of physical healing, and those of the healer became less appropriate to the task of spiritual direction and instruction.

Quite reasonably, today we are inclined to believe that this distinction between the functions of healer and priest was an important *discovery* and not merely a new and different way to construct reality. Something that we might call "human disease" thus emerged. In a critical realistic perspective, this category both marked the discovery of a new dimension of human experience and justified (or created) that dimension. To say that the category *created* the new dimension is to emphasize the social constructionist side of the emerging awareness, that is, that medicine was *constructed* for a social purpose. But this view should be balanced, according to critical realism, with the supposition that there was a pre-existing dimension of reality (human disease) awaiting discovery by the category. In this critical realist view, thereafter there will always be a functional correspondence between the category and the discovered reality. Thus, a new human enterprise had emerged.

Returning to the main point, the claim that psychology is a truly original and unique explanatory language developed to name an aspect of human experience not previously named implies an historical research process that brings to light, rather than constructs, a reality. That it has occurred in the context of and in response to certain social and political circumstances is also true and important, as Foucault has argued.[6]

But to regard psychology exclusively as a product of social construction, reflecting primarily the needs and exigencies current at the time of its origin, is erroneous and could result in the discipline's demise. Perhaps this would not be a significant problem if it were shared by all sciences. But sciences having longer histories are not so regarded by their own practitioners nor by others. Consider the impact on physics of viewing it only as a product of social construction. Calculations of the acceleration of balls rolling down incline planes or of trajectories of planets within a star system need to presuppose the reality of those balls, planes, planets, and stars as well as of more abstract entities like incline planes and trajectories. Einsteinian accounts of the universe superseded those of Newton not because Newton was wrong, but because he was not as inclusive of observed data and because Einstein began to ask somewhat new and different questions about the reality. To explain either Newton or Einstein's physics merely as a response to social/political/economic forces would be misleading.

However, psychologists and nonpsychologists sometimes believe that psychology represents nothing really new, but is a repackaging of philosophy, biomedicine, educational theory, and religion. Why this difference between physics and psychology? One reason, already alluded to, is that physics has a longer history and thus has higher public credibility as an independent and respectable scientific endeavor. A more penetrating reason is the western cultural bias that physical science deals with what is "real," namely the material realm, while psychology, like religion, deals with what is much more elusive and less "real," namely the spiritual and interpersonal realm.

Some Popular Philosophical Assumptions

This ascription of greater reality to physical phenomena than to spiritual or psychic phenomena is hard to counter effectively, or even be fully cognizant of, since our culture subscribes to it so implicitly.[7] But it is well to remember much of the popular impetus of early psychology came from the assertion by New Thought advocates, like Mary Baker Eddy and Anton Mesmer, that the mind has at least the same level of reality as does the physical realm (Meyer 1980).[8] There is a sense in which psychologists continue to be the primary modern-day champions of this position; they should not fall prey to the pervasive cultural/philosophical presuppositions that tend to undermine this belief. In fact, belief in the mind as having an ontological status equal to that of matter is one way to refer to psychology's central idea.

It is true that philosophic positions among psychologists vary on this general issue of ontology with respect to psychological phenomena, partly depending on how philosophically inclined they happen to be. But this difference of opinion should not affect psychology's commitment to the mind as *equal* to matter even if a particular ontology may question commonsense assumptions about physical or mental reality. In this more sophisticated understanding of what is real, *both* mind and matter can be assigned some meaning that differs from that provided by a naive common sense without affecting the equality of their standing.

Nor do I propose any downgrading of the significance of physical reality, as advocated in the nineteenth century by such influential New Thought advocates as Mary Baker Eddy, the founder of Christian Science. Eddy elevated the mind, probably in reaction to a growing cultural materialism, to a status well above that of matter, so much so that matter was actually trivialized. This assertion is reminiscent of the gnosticism and docetism of some early Christian thinkers who denied the reality or importance of the flesh. These were branded as heretical in the early church. But denial of the physical world has never seriously afflicted the discipline of psychology, which has neurobiology as an ongoing central concern and one of its important historical roots. And such denial would be ironic in light of psychology's close self-modeling after the physical sciences. For several decades after the turn of this century, academic psychology expressed its genuine and deep interest in the physical basis of mental life through countless experiments on neural conductivity, reaction time, localization of brain functions, and, more recently, the mechanisms of neurotransmission and biochemistry of neurotransmitters. Introductory textbooks in psychology typically feature an early chapter on biology to provide the student up-to-date information in this area. All of this reflects a healthy respect for the body in human mental activity.

INVOLVEMENT OF THE MIND/BODY ISSUE

When the mind and body are compared in importance, the age-old mind/body problem is automatically revisited. There is not space here to review the arguments for the various monist, dualist, or tripartite positions. Suffice it to say that the currently ascendant position among psychologists is a working body/mind monism in which biological and mental issues interact in such a closely intertwined way that it is considered impractical and/or impossible to extricate one from the other. It is important to note that the language of interaction, however, unavoidably continues to imply a dualism; it does not, as is sometimes assumed, eliminate the problem. To speak of an interaction presumes separate entities that interact. Despite its official lack of academic respectability, the dualism in the daily thought of even well-trained psychologists probably persists because the categories of physical versus nonphysical run deep and are fundamental to our common cultural way of understanding reality. I believe there is a fundamental difference between mind and body, but I also know that the two are inseparable because I cannot truly understand the activity of one without considering the activity of the other.[9]

Rather than lament this return to a form of dualism, it would be better for us to frankly recognize with philosopher of science Michael Polanyi (1958) that theorizing is deeply personal and involves core beliefs and presuppositions that can be defended only partially by the reasoning process.[10] The Dutch philosopher Herman Dooyeweerd (1953) went even further by asserting that the theoretical enterprise is religious at its core in the sense that it both inevitably and legitimately tends to reflect the most deeply held values of the theorist and the theorizing community; therefore, theorizing with integrity both recognizes the impact of these values on one's theory and consistently expresses them throughout the theorizing process. The truth is that our culture in general and psychologists in particular value a belief in what has been called variously mental, psychic, or spiritual reality, or, stated negatively, that aspect of reality that is not physical/biological. In psychology's notorious attempt to ape the natural sciences at various points it has been tempted, and has sometimes succumbed to the temptation, to sell its birthright and critical belief in the mind for the current views of the culture.

THE BROADER PHILOSOPHICAL ISSUE OF MATERIALISM

While denial of physical reality has never afflicted the discipline of psychology, denial of mental reality has been a serious problem at times and continues to be so today. The most famous and serious challenge came from John B. Watson, the founder of behaviorism. His antimentalist views dominated psychology for several decades. Even the cognitive revolution beginning in the 1950s was treated as a threat by some, and its advocates had to carefully assure the psychological community that it did not represent a return to the blatant dualism espoused by Titchener and other early dualistic psychologists. Psychologists trained after Watson, and especially B. F. Skinner, have been strongly defensive about the reality of mind, so that self theorists in the psychoanalytic tradition and third-force psychologists such as Carl Rogers and Abraham Maslow were clearly accorded second-class citizenship in academic circles through the 1960s. As indicated above, the subsequent cognitive revolution has provided a kind of permission for therapists and personality theorists at least to communicate meaningfully with those for whom belief in a real mind continues to be anathema.

Historically, antimentalism is closely linked with materialism. The word *materialism* will be used here in the classic philosophical sense that each and every mental and spiritual event results only from physical processes (*Britannica* Vol. 7, 929). That the basic issues are perennial and philosophical in nature and go back much further than the debates within psychology is well illustrated in the following dialogue between Socrates and Theaetetus, recorded by Socrates' student Plato in *Sophist*:

> *Socrates:* What we shall see is something like a Battle of Gods and Giants going on between them over their quarrel about reality.
> *Theaetetus:* How so?
> *Socrates:* One party is trying to drag everything down to earth out of heaven and the unseen, literally grasping rocks and trees in their hands; for they lay hold upon every stock and stone and strenuously affirm that real existence belongs only to that which can be handled and offers resistance to the touch. They define reality as the same thing as body, and as soon as one of the opposite party asserts that anything without a body is real, they are utterly contemptuous and will not listen to another word.
> *Theaetetus:* The people you describe are certainly a formidable crew. I have met quite a number of them before now.
> *Socrates:* Yes, and accordingly their adversaries are very wary in defending their position somewhere in the heights of the unseen, maintaining with all their force that true reality consists in certain intelligible and bodiless Forms. In the clash of argument they shatter and pulverise those bodies which their opponents wield, and what those others allege to be

true reality they call, not real being, but a sort of moving process of becoming. On this issue an interminable battle is always going on between the two camps (qtd. in Grossman 1992, vii).

One implication of the "battle" described by Socrates is the difficulty of attributing equal ontological standing to mind and matter. Historically, such a belief seems unstable and tends to resolve itself toward a monism of either mind or matter. Why this may be true is not clear, but conventional historical analysis seems to bear it out. In the Western world, eras when the general culture emphasizes this present world with its material reality alternate with eras that emphasize a transcendent world with a *meta*-physical reality. Thus the Greek Golden Age, with its stress on ideas and ideals, turned into the Roman period, with its stress on material pleasure and world domination. Later, the medieval period stressed mental/ spiritual values but gradually gave way to a cultural preoccupation in the Renaissance with the beauty and intricacies of human and natural physical reality. We must not forget that it was in the Renaissance that modern science was born. Psychology as a discipline has both reflected and shaped some of these briefer alternating emphases.

The popular movement of mind cure, such as New Thought and Mesmerism, that set the stage for psychology's development, was clearly an attempt to construe mental power as directly analogous to, and equal in importance to, material energy. Some major representatives of these movements, like Mary Baker Eddy, were explicit in their teaching of the relationship between mind and matter. For example, in her book titled *Retrospection and Introspection*, Eddy says, "I gained the scientific certainty that all causation was Mind, and every effect a mental phenomenon." (qtd. in Titus 1953, 25).

Freud's doctrine of libidinal energy is another representative effort. Having noted the development of physics, and especially physical laws regarding transfer of energy within closed physical systems, Freud developed his ideas about the movement of libido from one part of a child's body to another; he taught that this movement of libido causes stage-wise changes in the child's basic personality needs. Libido is most simply understood as a kind of mental energy, notwithstanding the materialism usually ascribed to Freud (1905/1953).

Because they treated mental events in a scientific manner, these movements and theories were sometimes misinterpreted as a capitulation to the growing philosophic materialism of the late nineteenth century. However, these theories are better interpreted as a form of protest against materialism because, using scientific or quasi-scientific methods and language, they affirmed mind as having coequal status with matter. As noted above, it was largely from this protest against materialism that psychology was born. [11]

This emphasis on mind over matter, or mind *equal* to matter, was not just characteristic of people and movements that prefigured academic psychology. Early prominent figures within academic psychology itself, such as Franz Brentano and Gustav Fechner, were vigorous champions of the reality of mind. Brentano was a Roman Catholic priest who never renounced the core of his theological beliefs, including the reality of mind/ spirit, but whose psychological ideas greatly impressed many of his contemporaries, including Freud himself. In discussing the influence of Brentano, David Murray (1988) says, "Brentano's emphasis on the mental [as opposed to the physiological as stressed by Wundt] was echoed by various other Austrian writers whose indebtedness to Brentano was, however, less direct than that of Stumpf and Husserl," (273) Brentano stressed the experiencing mind in which an encapsulated event, an act, occurred.

Similarly, Murray (1988) writes of Fechner that his later quasi-mystical works attempted to show that "consciousness . . . could be seen as an indissoluble property of all things, so that instead of only viewing mind as an epiphenomenon of body, *bodies could also be viewed as epiphenomena of mind.*" [emphasis added] (81) Likewise, current historians of psychology generally believe that Wilhelm Wundt's *Volkpsychologie*, in which he views the person as a proactive player within a given social context, was not taken as seriously as were his more physiologically modeled structuralist formulations nor as seriously as he would have liked.

The American pioneer psychologist William James also expressed some ambivalence about the existence of mind or self although, as Gordon Allport (1961) notes in the following paragraph, his major tendency was to affirm it:

> This issue has worried many, perhaps most, philosophers, but not all of them reach the same conclusion. The philosopher Hume, for example, concluded

reluctantly and with no strong sense of conviction, that a continuing agent (a self) was more of an illusion than a fundamental fact. He decided that men are made up of discrete bits of experience. William James—wrestling with the same problem—concluded that there is no single cementing principle but that unity lies in the overlap of successive states and acts, much as the unity of a shingled roof consists of the overlay of shingles. (378)

These successive states and acts comprise what James calls the stream of consciousness.

BEHAVIORISM AS A MOMENTOUS DETOUR

The decisive events in turning psychology away from belief in mind came through the powerful movement later called *behaviorism*. The influence of behaviorism began with John B. Watson in the 1920s and lasted 30 to 40 years.[12] It was a fundamental deviation from psychology's core idea that, in the evolving empirical discipline of psychology, a truly unique explanatory language had developed to name and understand an aspect of human experience that had never been named or understood before.

Behaviorism tried to replace psychology as an original language describing human experience in a fundamentally new way, but it could not. Instead, it became the positivistic application of the biological idea of *tropism* to human experience. It borrowed an idea directly from biology with little of the modification needed to adjust to its new subject matter.

In fact, even tropism itself was not quite at the center of the behaviorist revolt: Methodology was at the center. In effect, behaviorism attempted to substitute the core idea that focused on biological methodology as psychology's defining characteristic. This meant that the discipline of psychology would subsequently be defined as that human discipline in which, above all, rigorous *scientific methods* are applied to individual human experience. The notion of studying the mind as psychology's core idea was supplanted by placing methodology at the center of the discipline, with biological tropism as the most important corollary.

This question of what constitutes the most scientific of the available range of empirical methods became the issue at stake. Are approaches that sacrifice precision, detail, and exquisitely operationalized definitions less scientific than those that stress them? Behaviorism answered "yes" to this.

In fact, Watson was importing from biology an unmodified, *a priori* assumption about the nature of scientific methods. The idea of tropism perfectly expressed this assumption.

One of Watson's teachers, Jacques Loeb (1918), had taken pains to emphasize that plants cannot properly be understood as intending to grow toward the light or toward a water supply. These are "teleological" ideas, ascribing intentionality to the plant, and therefore unaccceptable. Teleological theory was branded "vitalism"—the idea that the plant has a life principle within that directs its course. Instead, said Loeb, plants bend toward both light and water as a result of the operation of a cause-and-effect chain from the past by means of differential cellular growth patterns that immediately cause functional "movement" by the plant. So, too, positivism reasoned by direct analogy, human behavior cannot properly be understood teleologically but always as a tropistic outcome, the consequence of a chain of cause-and-effect events from the past.

To Watson and many others, this seemed to be the most scientifically plausible formulation of psychology's new direction for an era in which social science would be applied with astounding results to all of the most intransigent chronic human problems. It was an age of unfettered optimism, and that optimism's name was *science*. More recently, this view has been called both simplistic and scientistic.

Because among the earliest psychologists the use of empirical methodology had been an important tenet of the discipline, this behavioristic redefinition of psychology did not immediately appear to be the significant deviation from its identity that it truly was. In the 1920s milieu of optimism about social science's potential to solve our problems, behaviorism was widely hailed as a welcome refinement in psychology's modern redefinition. In fact, it represented a subtle shift to a scientistic focus on methods rather than on the only worthy focus of psychological science, the person.[13]

PSYCHOANALYSIS: ONE GUARDIAN OF PSYCHOLOGY'S LEGACY

Within traditional psychology, the subdiscipline that has been most true to the idea of psychology has been psychoanalysis. While the initial form proposed by Freud was closely associated with and derived directly from biological assumptions—it assumed the instinctual aggressive and sexual drive as the basis of all behavior—the object relations and self theory forms that developed shortly thereafter were almost entirely independent of biology.[14] Though Freud strenuously maintained that biological instincts were essential to his theory, the foundations of these two formulations were already present in Freud's theory, in the view of those who formulated them and who regard themselves as quite loyal to the master's insights.

Because several generations of psychiatrists were trained in psychoanalysis, Freud's theories are often considered the foundation of the medical model in thinking about both abnormal and normal behavior. While the medical establishment did indeed pre-empt diagnosis and treatment of psychological disorders, psychoanalysis did about as much as could be done in nineteenth-century and early twentieth-century Europe and America to affirm mind, albeit a largely subconscious one, as a worthy focus of investigation at the core of human experience. It is significant that Freud supported the training of lay analysts (nonphysicians) although most of his followers held out for a medical degree as a prerequisite to the practice of psychoanalysis. Freud did not regard training in medicine as essential to understanding the application of his theories.

It is ironic that the physician Freud should propose one of the most thoroughly psychological theories available to psychologists today. That it is indeed a thoroughly psychological theory is arguably one of its strongest continuing lures, perhaps even exceeding its technical or therapeutic value. The enormously complex nature of psychoanalytic theorizing makes this point better than any specific tenet of the theory. That is, when the complicated maneuverings of the mind are described and analyzed with typical psychoanalytic self-assuredness, among the definite meta-messages that are conveyed are that mind exists, and it is amenable to investigation.

Consider this passage concerning the self theory of H. Kohut by Eagle and Wolitzky (1992):

> According to Freud, normal development is characterized by a *decreasing* investment of libido in the ego and an *increasing* investment of libido in the object. In short, according to traditional theory, in normal development we move from self love to object love (although Freud noted that a certain

minimal degree of self love is necessary for psychological health). Further-more, given the limited supply of libido, there is a *reciprocal* relation between self interest and object interest. Too much absorption in the self is necessarily at the expense of interest in the other, and conversely, too much absorption in the other is at the expense of the interest of the self. (137)

A theorist who does not want to attribute reality to a mere linguistic formulation will normally make every effort to stay close to operational definitions that are experimentally testable. Psychoanalysts and their fol-lowers notoriously violate this elementary convention and instead go on at length about the ins and outs of mental functioning, to the clear discom-fort of most nonpsychoanalytic psychologists. Eagle and Wolitzky's ex-ample, written in 1992, is not nearly as technically tangled and obscure as is much abstruse psychoanalytic theorizing.

Why do psychoanalysts do this? Where do they find the liberty to speculate endlessly and self-confidently about the parts of the personality, early formative experiences, and the effect of current significant influences? And why are they not also constrained by the positivist assumptions that have ruled most psychological theorizing and that require evidence to support every assertion?

The answer is simply that the nineteenth-century assumption con-cerning the genuine reality of mind is implicit and remains deeply in-grained in psychoanalysis and its derivative forms. Although he considered himself thoroughly secularized, Freud is now generally understood to have been vastly influenced by the Talmudic Jewish tradition; the preservation of personal mental life may well have been one consequence of this influ-ence. Ironically, even those psychologists not especially charmed by psy-choanalysis but who wish to conserve a sense of individual mind as the core psychological idea remain attracted to, and perhaps grateful for, the psychoanalytic tradition. It is because that tradition has somehow had the courage, perhaps as an extension of Freud's own audacity, to conserve a cultural belief that was, and is, under siege.[15]

Cognitive Theory as a Move Toward Affirming Mind

Although the dominance of behaviorism over much of the discipline of psychology, as noted above, represents a long hiatus in official psychology's endorsement of mind, the "cognitive revolution" during the last three decades has been well documented by several writers as a plausible road back to the notion of mind for psychology (Evans 1977). However, rehabilitating the concept of mind is a slow process because the kind of mentalism that developed in the first decades of psychology's infancy tends to short-circuit any scientific investigative process. In the same way that the instinct theory of McDougall (1912) and others provides only a pseudo-explanation by simply labeling specific behaviors as expressions of particular instincts, mentalism attributes action patterns to mental tendencies or faculties.

This exercise of naming the instinct behind every behavior seemed intellectually sound to McDougall but was gradually understood as a tautological, and therefore empty, explanatory exercise. Similarly, it came to be believed that no genuine progress in explanation can be made by simply attributing a behavioral phenomenon to a homunculus within—a person called "mind" within the person. This attribution, it was said, is an infinitely regressive drill that does not enable authentic explanation, control, or prediction of behavior, although it may at times *sound* scientific. Watson (1914) and others argued that like instinct, mind is a pseudo-explanation.

Typically, psychologists within the current cognitive revolution, although taking great pains to renounce any return on their part to the discredited mentalism of the first decades of this century, nonetheless express dissatisfaction as well with the explanatory power of traditional learning theory. The positivist physicalism that became normative from the 1920s through the 1950s resulted in a proliferation of experimental studies on numerous aspects of the learning process, including Pavlovian and operant conditioning as well as properties of learning predicted by broad-based theories such as those of Clark Hull (1952) and Kenneth Spence (1956).[16] But a crisis of dissatisfaction with these mainstream studies developed in the late 1950s and the 1960s as some critics inside and outside psychology's ranks pronounced the mainstream discipline interesting but irrelevant.

The critical task of the new cognitive psychologist was to show due appreciation for the learning theory tradition and its disdain for the old mentalism while demonstrating that a chastened return to investigating "the black box"—all the complex intricacies of mental life that result in actions—is in the interest of psychology as a discipline. How these young psychologists of the 1960s and later were able to make their case plausible has yet to be adequately chronicled by historians of psychology, but there is no doubt that they have been successful. The result is a mini-paradigmatic shift for the field and a partial resurgence of confidence in mind as a legitimate focus of scientific investigation.

An even bolder assertion of mind has recently appeared within official psychology in our own day in the work of George Howard (1996) and his associates at Notre Dame University. They explore the issue of human volition—a topic long considered unscientific because it is not amenable to standard social scientific methodology. Nonetheless, volition has long been held philosophically as at the core of human mental processes (mind) and is a far cry from the tropism of Jacques Loeb and John Watson. Howard's groundbreaking work is an extraordinarily clever effort to show that a scientific psychology can include within its scope a set of concepts suggestive of the exercise of personal free choice—something not considered possible until now and still rejected by many.

WHAT DIFFERENCE DOES PSYCHOLOGY'S SELF-DEFINITION REALLY MAKE?

What consequential difference, in theory or practice, would result from clarifying the nature of the psychological enterprise by giving *mind* its proper central place as the focus of theory and research? Would such a change result in an exclusion of some topics currently included in psychology's domain, topics such as neuropsychology or developmental, pharmacological, and even social psychology? Further, would some professional groups, [such as physicians (psychiatrists), clergy, or social workers,] be excluded from making use of psychology?

The short answer is uniformly "no." Any topic currently taught and considered relevant or ancillary to psychology in meaning and/or practical significance should not be ignored. Understanding the anatomy and neurophysiology of the central nervous system is obviously advantageous to the psychologist because it is axiomatic among psychologists that "everything psychological is simultaneously biological." (Myers 1995, 41) And it is clear that early experience is formative in shaping later mental life. Similar remarks could be made about the meaning of our social experiences.

But construing the human mind again as truly the major focus of psychology's labor will cast a different light on each of these supplementary areas of study (i.e., supplementary in relation to psychology). Each area will find its own orbit around the study of mind, but no one of them should ever be mistaken as a serious contender for psychology's primary focus.

Because of the prevailing social constructionist definition of psychology, a type of academic anarchy currently reigns in which the various subdisciplines of psychology more or less follow independent courses of research and theorizing. In this milieu of pluralism, the supreme value is tolerance combined with a reticence to critically utilize any criterion except methodology to assess the lasting contributions made by the subdisciplines. As it is, a worker in a given sub-area of psychology looks at researchers in other sub-areas with a bemused curiosity, much as an astronomer might view the work of a biologist. They do not sufficiently acknowledge a single and powerful unifying theme.

It does seem that this situation is changing. In recent years the idea of psychology formulated during the reign of behaviorism has been broadened. The standard definition of psychology through those several decades (i.e., the scientific study that seeks to understand, predict, and control human behavior) has been broadened, as in one popular introductory psychology textbook, to include more than bare behavior: "the science of behavior *and* mental processes." [emphasis added] (Myers 1995, 2) While this is clearly an improvement over a focus merely on observable behavior, it suggests an underlying duality that tends to subvert a unified, integrated purpose. Why cannot the study of "mental processes" as easily include the study of behavior, just as the study of "behavior" was considered for many decades inclusive of mental processes?

A closer look at the newer definition reveals that its two parts, on the one hand, *behavior* and, on the other, *mental processes*, correspond to the classic mind/body dualism so deeply ingrained in Western thought and language. This is no accident. The threefold influence of currently popular psychology, psychoanalysis, and the cognitive revolution has forced a concession to mental processes within formal psychology. This concession, in turn, is undoubtedly related to the sense of promises un-fulfilled as we approach both the century's end and psychology's century-and-a-quarter birthday. So we are now in the process of deciding whether psychology is primarily about bodies acting (directed by brains); spirits ruling (influenced by other spirits); or human minds thinking, feeling, valuing, choosing, and, yes, acting. This necessary choice in no way implies a demeaning or disapproval of biology and the burgeoning brain science that has recently astounded the world with discovery after amazing discovery. Nor does it imply any lack of respect or appreciation for theo-logical and spiritual truth. What it does imply is that if the scope of psychology is more intentionally circumscribed, its theoretical and exper-imental efforts will more meaningfully take their place in a maturing science.

TOWARD CORRECTING PSYCHOLOGY'S MISDIRECTION: EXTERNAL INFLUENCES

The thesis set forth in this book is that the discipline of psychology would be stronger and healthier if it were organized around and integrated by means of a single emphasis on mind. Many of the challenges to this central theme have been already briefly explored in this chapter. But so far the opponents to this central idea in psychology's history have been represented as having exercised their influence *within* the discipline, rather than out-side it. That is, I have considered the constraints operating from inside the discipline that have resulted in the excessive pluralism and identity diffusion that characterize psychology at the end of the 1990s.

In some ways, it will be more profitable to consider the external social factors that have produced this critical problem in self-definition, because, like an adolescent in identity crisis, externalizing the enemy—specifying the external concomitants of unwelcome identity elements—sometimes helps to formulate a remedial plan. Such an analysis in no way exonerates psychology itself from responsibility for its less-than-meaning-ful digressions, but recognizes that its drift away from a central organizing idea also may be considered a consequence of acceding to the expectations and demands of other influential social groups. In the absence of a strong, mature identity, psychology may have accommodated its purpose and mission to other strong cultural voices.

STRONG EXTERNAL VOICES

The first of these voices to be considered is theology and its popular spokespersons, who are inclined to redefine psychology in terms of spiritual/moral/theological categories rather than, as I defined it above, a unique explanatory language that has developed to name and understand an aspect of human experience that *has never been named or understood before.* Theology would say that, in fact, psychology has been named and understood before, by theology. Purporting to be a truly alternative conceptual language to theology in accounting for human experience, psychology constitutes a major challenge to theology and the spiritual establishment in its many varying forms. This establishment includes, but is not limited to, the world's great religions as well as newer religious movements like New Age.

It is not always the leaders and religious functionaries who feel most threatened by psychology; they are often better educated and therefore recognize that theology really cannot be replaced by any social science. Rather, the opposition often comes from lay practitioners, who are more inclined to see psychologists as the new priesthood. Overall, religion has been one of the major social impediments to psychology's strong self-definition, and many unfortunate, compromising alliances have been made with religion. To theology, mind is functionally equivalent to spirit, making psychology a competing and antagonistic perspective on the same basic human experiences. I will address this external voice in chapter 2.

Biology and medicine comprise the second of these powerful cultural voices. If theology has tried to absorb psychology, so have neurology, psychiatry, and the medical establishment. That psychology offers a conceptual language different from and as radically fundamental as that of neurons, chemicals, drugs, and various states of brain tissue in making sense of human life is to some incomprehensible and presumptuous in the extreme.

In the exciting atmosphere of burgeoning knowledge within brain science, where research moves forward rapidly in neuro-cognitive psychology, artificial intelligence, and computer science in addition to the traditional medical fields of neurology and psychiatry, the temptation to equate mind and brain is almost irresistible. Again, professional researchers and practitioners of brain sciences are often more willing to acknowledge psychology's distinct contribution than are less informed members of the public. To the latter, it is regressive and "unscientific" to believe that what we now crudely call psychology will not one day be totally reduced to the science of neurons, neurotransmitters, cortical localizations, and physical/drug interventions.[17] In this view of biology, mind is functionally equivalent to brain; the two terms are sometimes used interchangeably. As with theology, some psychologists become unintentional confederates with neurology's unwarranted hegemony in the interest of inclusiveness and tolerant pluralism. I will address this external voice in chapter 3.

Psychology's effort to take its rightful place, then, has been chiefly hindered by theological and medical reluctance to recognize its distinctive sphere of discourse. These ancient crafts have not been hospitable to the professional newcomer. This war has been, and continues to be, fought on many fronts. It is essential that psychologists recognize what is at stake and refrain from inadvertently undermining psychology's own purpose.

Two other less serious threats to psychology's idea will be addressed in this book. These are the disciplines of social work and education.

LESSER EXTERNAL VOICES

Social work needs to be distinguished carefully from psychology, both for practical and theoretical reasons. The discipline of social work is conceptually different from psychology, religion, and medicine in that, within its framework, the individual is always understood primarily as a member of one or more social groups. The sociological perspective of an organismic group life that can be studied somewhat independently of its constituent individual members and that "determines" their behavior precludes mind from being a *primary* focus of social work. Any group, large or small, has a life of its own, and social work purports to understand the individual as a participant in this group life.

Such a perspective on the individual is invaluable as it supplements the study of mind. Whether groups can meaningfully have existence or ontological status equal with spirit, body, and mind is a philosophical question to be addressed elsewhere. Currently, our culture is inclined to hold the viewpoint medicine teaches, the primacy of *body/brain* functions in understanding behavior, with mental, spiritual, and social explanations supplementing those explanations. I am asserting that psychology, rightly understood, affirms the primacy of *mental* functions in understanding behavior, with physical, spiritual, and social explanation supplementing those explanations. This assertion is not imperialistic; it is essential to psychology's core idea.

Is there a serious likelihood that an individual will be construed exclusively as a unit of a group? That is, in a social work perspective, would mind be ignored? Not much, in our current cultural milieu. But, as we will see in chapter 4, historically several notable attempts have been made to establish that very premise; it will be important for psychologists to learn to value the social work perspective for what it can offer along these lines, rather than for what it cannot by itself provide.

Although none of the book's chapters is dedicated to education, I feel it is important here to mention the tendency to reduce psychology's enterprise to an educational project. In this case, the notion of mind becomes functionally equivalent to "knowledge base." Because it is in possession of, and has access to, knowledge, either for problem-solving or goal-seeking, the formal educational enterprise is sometimes mistakenly considered inclusive of all of psychology's basic purposes. It does not recognize the claim of "a truly original explanatory language that has developed to name and understand an aspect of human experience that has never been named or understood before."

Historically, we can see this confusion in the tendency of some universities to house psychology departments within departments of education as well as the common policy of requiring that undergraduate educational psychology courses be taught by education professionals rather than by psychologists. In these cases, students are encouraged to see psychology as a branch of education.

It is important to reiterate that I do not intend to belittle the human educational endeavor. Education is another ancient and venerable profession whose practitioners should have no anxiety about ever being replaced. Because education is not currently a truly serious threat to psychology's identity search, I will not focus on it in this book.

Now I turn to an attempt to circumscribe the role of psychology in today's academic and professional world by comparing and contrasting psychology to those disciplines with which it is most likely to be confused at the beginning of the twenty-first century. I hope that psychology's work in the new century will be enhanced by a renewed economy of effort, as it confidently declines to entangle itself in tasks and issues that have little to do with its central concern.

NOTES

1. This tendency for radical social movements, both religious and secular, to become socially respectable with the passage of time accounts, for example, for the Communist Party of Russia becoming the party of the conservatives in the late 1990s!

2. Thus, Freedheim (1992) shows that in the early 1960s when Rollo May sensed that psychotherapists who were not medical doctors were in danger of being legally outlawed in New York, he gathered a group of psychotherapists that included psychiatrists, psychologists, social workers, ministers, and educators. He made common cause with them to establish the acceptability of non-medical psychotherapy.

3. In some ways it was unfortunate that Sigmund Freud was a medical doctor. There is nothing intrinsic to his theory that is essentially physicalistic, although he tended to think in physical categories appropriate to his training. His assumptions were materialist, but his theory can be fully understood in psychological concepts. His genius was to be a pioneer in a discipline that was neither medicine nor theology.

4. The birth of psychology is usually dated from Wilhelm Wundt's establishing of a psychological laboratory in Leipzig, Germany, in 1879. By this widely recognized event psychology has traditionally affirmed that a genuinely new human enterprise was beginning that was not merely an extension of its parents, biology and philosophy.

5. I am defining "critical realism" somewhat narrowly. Philosophers in the tradition of Karl Popper (1959) have carefully elucidated this position without implying that it is the only way to view the structure of human knowledge. These questions, of course, go back to the differences between Plato and Aristotle

on the question of how real is that which we perceive and know. Critical realism is in contrast to the more social reconstructionist positions of some psychologists like Kenneth Gergin (1985) and R. Harre (1984), who have argued that the meaning of psychological concepts mostly depends on the social/political context in which they are presented.

6. Foucault (1988) has provided a trenchant analysis of the development of therapeutic psychology in response to the social and political realities of Europe and the United States at the end of the nineteenth century.

7. This "two worlds" view goes back at least to Greek philosophers like Plato. But Plato saw even the physical realm as a shadowy reflection on the cave wall of ideal forms from a transcendent realm. Thus he taught that the ideal form, the idea, has a more fundamental and permanent reality than the actual object.

8. Also, this history is nicely detailed by Philip Cushman in "Psychotherapy to 1992: A Historically Situated Interpretation" (Freedheim 1992).

9. This issue is best considered as a quest for a way to understand the full array of human experience. If we find that in day-by-day practice we cannot consistently maintain the monistic position in our work and thought about psychology, then it is worth re-evaluating dualism as a working hypothesis.

10. Thus, professional philosophers may find the problems with dualism so severe as to render it untenable, while psychologists may simultaneously find doing without some version of dualism virtually impossible.

11. The New Thought movement begun by Phineas P. Quimby (1802–1866) is a powerful popular reaction to scientific empiricism. It advocates mental and spiritual healing and teaches that illness is entirely a result of mental events. An international New Thought Alliance was formed in 1914 and continues today.

12. It is sometimes said that Behaviorism was defunct about 30 years after its founding. This may be true for most of philosophical scholarship, but I can testify that in psychology it was still a powerful force well into the 1970s. Neobehaviorism is currently a significant perspective in psychology.

13. For an incisive analysis of the loss of the person as a focus of modern psychology, see *The Person in Psychology* by Mary Stuart Van Leeuwen (1985).

14. This point is forcefully made by Morris Eagle and David Wolitzky, "Psychoanalytic Theories of Psychotherapy," in *History of Psychotherapy: A Century of Change* (Freedheim 1992, 126ff).

15. Curiously, the Department of Experimental Psychology at Cambridge University, England, has annually offered a course in psychoanalysis despite the

otherwise rigorously empirical bases of virtually all its other course offerings. This fact testifies to the remarkable robustness of psychoanalysis.

16. What was current thinking among psychologists in the decades of the 1920s through the 1950s, positivist physicalism, had already been abandoned by most philosophers as bankrupt. Although psychologists as a group are more philosophically informed than their psychiatric and other natural science colleagues, they still tend to be somewhat out-of-date. This is, of course, not always disadvantageous.

17. This is a view philosophers call "eliminative reductionism." In this kind of reductionism, the higher emergent discipline is likely to be replaced eventually by the parent discipline (e.g., biology would be replaced by chemistry). This view is not taken very seriously by philosophers, but popular writers, many psychiatrists, and a few psychologists hold this expectation and shape their research programs around fulfilling it.

2

Psychology in Contrast with Religion

*W*e turn now to consider how the general failure of psychology to define its boundaries clearly, and to discipline itself to stay within them in its research, theorizing, and applications, has resulted in a general confusion about the differences between religious and psychological concepts. This confusion is illustrated by some prominent theologians who, without caution, developed theologies that are virtually pseudopsychologies, and by some prominent psychologists who readily took the role of secular priests, a role our society in turn began to assign to them.[1]

These infractions represented failures to treat boundaries of conceptual disciplines with sufficient respect. On this matter, recall the major foundational point of philosopher Herman Dooyeweerd (1953) that each science has its own *Geganstand* [peculiar standpoint], which is different from that of each other individual science. No scientific field holds any primacy in this respect. It is, he believed, philosophy that integrates various unique standpoints into a coherent, integrated whole. He and I seek an overview that can clarify contributions of individual disciplines.

Historically, the generative powers from which seedling psychological ideas later developed have been ascribed to the fields of religion, philosophy, and biology. Perhaps because of the vast differences among these parent disciplines, psychology was torn in several directions, having incompletely differentiated itself from its parents, thus making disciplinary "fences" difficult to honor. Even today psychological theorists tacitly express allegiances to biology, philosophy, or religion in the stances they take on perennial issues; their failure to realize this fact sometimes results in blurred boundaries between psychology and these disciplines.

Such blurred boundaries exacerbate rather than reduce competitive relations between disciplines, making the relationship between them and psychology complex. Territorial skirmishes have developed. Psychologists are thought to have one of the lowest rates of religious belief among all the professions. As psychology expresses antagonism toward religion for a range of reasons, we begin to suspect that the excessive protests are psychology's attempt to prove to itself that the historical umbilical cord to religion has indeed been cut.

Similarly, religionists often have refused to acknowledge many important ideas as innovative psychological discoveries, insisting instead that they were to be found in the core of traditional religion all along. Trying to include psychology within its own sphere of discourse and authority, religion has been slow to recognize psychology's independent status. Theology, broadly defined, is surely the most ancient contender for the job of making sense of human life and experience. Since time out of mind, behavior, feelings, attitudes, and possible interactions with the gods and with other spiritual beings have been interpreted by priests, prophets, clairvoyants, monks, sages, ministers, and a multitude of religiously gifted individuals. In any society, including our modern industrialized states, even people who deny any personal commitment to a religious viewpoint generally ascribe a degree of wisdom to those who have been accorded religious standing.

In the final analysis, whether we value any theology at all depends on whether we accept the existence, importance, and actual intervention of one or more supernatural beings. Simply stated, if people do not believe there are spirits or spiritual influences, they will likely believe that teachings about the spiritual are misleading or, at best, an anesthesia or emotional crutch that is rarely functional.

The fact that I do indeed accept the existence, importance, and actual interaction of supernatural beings with the world in real time in no way reduces my sense of the peril associated with religion's ongoing challenge to psychology's autonomy. My major concern here is that psychology not lose its authority as an independent and autonomous sphere of discourse in the sciences—that it not lose its *Geganstand*.

THE REASONS FOR CONFUSION

What we are considering here is the age-old reductionist effort of one intellectual area to swallow up another, to reduce another area to its own set of principles laid down within its own sphere. This effort involves examining methodological and presuppositional principles that are foundational to each sphere.

The question of whether there is a deliberate intention to be reductionist is always hard to answer.[2] It is easy to believe we have found deliberate reductionist efforts where in fact there has been no such design. It is more likely that most religionists are actually well intentioned and underinformed when they take psychological ideas and mistakenly reinterpret them in spiritual or theological terms. This inclination exemplifies the universal and functional human tendency to take what is new and perhaps threatening and, after comparing it with past experiences, make sense of it by reducing it to the old familiar categories at hand. Piaget (1977) calls it "assimilation."

When psychological concepts and methods seem familiar because they are analogous to those found in the religionists' own lexicon, it is natural for religionists to reduce the former to the latter. But when psychologists who ought to know better yield to the temptation to engage in this process, it may be professionally unethical and exploitative. It is particularly important for psychologists to be alert to this temptation if they are sympathetic to religion on other grounds. Those unsympathetic to religion need to be equally cautious not to overstep their social scientific authority by engaging in the negative evaluation of religious beliefs and practices.

In practice, psychologists both sympathetic and unsympathetic to various religious perspectives have not carefully avoided this temptation. Starting with Freud in *Totem and Taboo* (1913), *The Future of an Illusion* (1927), and *Moses and Monotheism* (1939), psychology has at times violated its discourse boundaries and devalued religion. Somewhat in deliberate opposition to Freud's position, Carl Jung isolated certain aspects of religious experience and gave them his tacit approval in works such as *Modern Man in Search of a Soul* (1933). William James also focused on religion in *The Varieties of Religious Experience* (1958), providing a qualified psychological support of religion for his generation. Gordon Allport's (1961) research on religious authenticity, although careful not to overtly judge religious beliefs, rates certain religious stances as superior to others from a mental health perspective.

In particular, recall Carl Jung's comment that first psychology lost its soul, then it lost its mind. This statement provides a clue to understanding the strong temptation for theologians and believing laypersons to assimilate psychology into spiritual teachings. Jung apparently lamented the eclipsing and replacement of religious teachings by dynamic psychology, and he did what he considered his part to remedy that error. He was one of the few modern psychologists—indeed, one of the few recent thinkers—who began to acknowledge the distinction between soul and mind (Ulanov 1975). This ancient distinction becomes crucial in separating the sphere of discourse in which psychology legitimately operates from that of theology or spirituality.[3]

For most modern people, it is difficult to maintain the dualism of mind and body, let alone attempt a tripartite usage of the terms body, mind, and spirit (or soul). However, this differential terminology ultimately defines the problem. If mind and spirit are two names for the same entity, then any sphere of discourse applying to the one may be used with the other, given some deft translation of terms respectively from one traditional sphere to the other. In this view, psychology becomes an empirically based undertaking to describe and explain the same phenomena that theology or religion in earlier times described and explained only on the basis of intuition and revelation—that is, nonscientifically.

The failure to differentiate spiritual and psychological terms results in a loss of complementarity and invariably generates an attitude of competition between the two fields. In the interest of making psychological findings more accessible to the religiously committed, popular writers or speakers who have taken two distinct concepts, one from religion and one from psychology, and rendered them functionally equivalent in order that they may be superimposed on each other, may be doing a disservice to their audience. I will give several examples presently, but one such is the best-selling author and psychiatrist M. Scott Peck, who has combined the moral, religious, and psychological domains so artfully that, for those who are spiritually inclined, the blend is nearly irresistible.[4]

Rendering two disparate concepts functionally equivalent causes the distinctive and salient elements of the concepts deriving from their respective domains to be lost. The benefit gained is ostensibly to tap the prestige and authority of the other field in the presentation of a grand integration. When this integration unites two fields that have as much current interest as psychology and spirituality, the results can be spectacular, accounting for the popularity of dozens of books and speaking tours. One reason is that many readers who maintain a serious interest in religion feel reassured that religion need not be abandoned in favor of science. A flavor of progress and modernity envelops what they have feared to be an outdated religious idea when it is translated into psychological terms.

Consider two examples. First, the ideas of guilt and forgiveness are commonly supposed to easily bridge the fields of psychology and religion such that psychologists are frequently asked to give their views on matters pertaining to human guilt. William James, Sigmund Freud, and many later psychologists have done so (James 1958; Freud, *The Future of an Illusion,* 1927). Similarly, priests, rabbis, ministers, mullahs, and religious of all kinds make pronouncements concerning guilt. It is a conceptual entity common to both psychology and religion.

Recall from chapter 1 the combined medical-religious ritual function of the biblical priest according to his mandate in Leviticus (chapter 13). Because the medical and religious spheres of discourse had not yet been differentiated, the priest's tasks included the diagnosis and treatment of skin diseases. This represents an immature stage of medicine's development. When medicine developed as an autonomous field, the priest's responsibility in the diagnosis and treatment of physical disease became purely ceremonial and secondary to his religious function.

Similarly, in the modern era a person's psychological response to a sense of having or performing wrong or evil thoughts or actions is gradually evolving as distinct from objective or ontological guilt. Ontological guilt refers to, and depends on, a moral standard existing outside the individual and believed by religious people to dwell in the fabric of the cosmos or in the mind of God. One's psychological, emotional, and behavioral response to a sense of having violated the moral standard, whether or not the violation actually occurred, is as discrete from real guilt as skin diseases are from a need for ritual purification.

It is misleading for psychology, *as* psychology, to speak about matters of ontological or moral guilt, just as the psychological experience of guilt should be of secondary importance to the religionist whose primary focus is moral conversion and integrity. It is the immaturity of psychology and the territoriality of religion that cloud or trivialize this important emerging differentiation.

To continue the example analysis, we might ask exactly what is lost in misusing the term *guilt* to mean both "guilty" responses (neurotic guilt, obsessive ruminations) and ontological guilt. What is so wrong in doing this? From the psychological viewpoint, mistakenly combining the two terms really implies that alleviation of guilty feelings and behaviors cannot happen separately from the removal of ontological guilt. But this is a mistake. Although we may personally prefer that ontological guilt removal normally accompany alleviation of guilty feelings and behaviors, psychologists can easily imagine instances in which the two phenomena are usefully separated, at least temporarily.[5]

In a parallel way, what is lost from a religious viewpoint results from the belief that the removal of ontological guilt cannot really happen apart from alleviating guilty feelings and behaviors. The two concepts—genuine guilt and guilty feelings—are mistakenly treated as functionally identical so that the elimination of guilty feelings becomes the goal. This is fallacious and misleading. In this confusion, forgiveness, atonement, propitiation—whatever the expression that means genuine guilt removal—is tied conceptually to the alleviation of certain feelings and behaviors, a confusion that undermines belief in, and understanding of, the objective forgiveness offered within most religious systems.

A second historical example of combining a concept from psychology and another from religion into a barren hybrid involves the idea of the very existence of God. Humanistic psychologists such as Carl Rogers (1961), Rollo May (1967), and Abraham Maslow (1968) teach that humans mentally construct or develop meaning in their lives and that this construction is close to the core of being human. This need for a sense of cosmic meaning then spawns some notion of a god or gods. Freud teaches something similar, although he ties that need for meaning closely to biological survival. The large body of Gestalt psychological research showing that human needs impose meaning on our environmental perceptions may also be interpreted as supporting Freud's conclusion. Gestaltists base their conclusion on the universality and persistent motivation of children and adults in every circumstance to generate personally satisfying pictures of the world from the experiences available to them.

The existential theologians of the 1950s through the 1970s, prominent among whom is Paul Tillich, teach that God may or may not exist as a person according to the usual and commonsense theological definition of that term.[6] But, Tillich (1963) teaches, this is of only limited concern because God surely exists if God is redefined as 1) "the ground of all being" and 2) that which a person values above all else. That is, if being is believed to have a foundation and if all people hold to a discoverable hierarchy of values, ranging from what they value least to what they value most, by definition God must exist.

The second of these assertions is what primarily concerns us here because of its obvious psychological nature. It is unlikely that such a definition for God would have been proposed or comprehended in any pre-existentialist or pre-psychological era, even by such an expert protopsychologist as Augustine, because it depends so heavily on the notion that each person generates "real" reality (ontology) within the everyday perceptual and conceptual process itself. The reality of God, his/her very existence, thus is generated along with all of the other meaningful constructs each person holds.

This rendering of the belief in God's existence as functionally equivalent in parallel psychological and theological terms seems at first to promise a gratifying integration. But it mutually cancels essential meanings across both spheres of discourse, leaving the final concept bereft of genuine meaning: God is a real comfort only if God exists, but God only exists if God is a real comfort. The marriage of psychology and religious creed is shown again to produce very questionable fruit.

As was true with the concept of guilt, there is a dual loss in redefining God using a concept that is both psychological and theological. The problem with this concept is that, from a religious viewpoint, God does not exist unless God is generated by the valuing person. This puts a severe strain on any traditional notion of God's existence, and, although not making the assertion false, it does call into question the ordinary meaning of the phrase "God exists." Then from a psychological viewpoint, we cannot really examine the authenticity of our own response to God's existence, unless the response happens to be patently psychotic, because God is not knowable apart from the valuing (psychological) process itself. This renders religious responses wholly idiosyncratic and not easily susceptible to evaluation. In effect, all psycho-religious responses become equally valid.

Clearly, here is a hopeless confusion of religious and psychological domains. What initially seemed to hold promise for an amalgam of important cross-discipline ideas results in the loss of vast amounts of meaning from each domain. This loss shows again how such modern theorists, both theologians and psychologists, overestimate the range of their concepts' applicability, failing to treat boundaries of conceptual disciplines with careful respect. Again recall the major foundational point of philosopher Herman Dooyeweerd, namely, the distinctive but equal *Geganstand* of each scientific discipline.

PRACTICAL RESULTS OF DISCIPLINARY CONFUSION

The problem is not merely of theoretical concern but has important pragmatic and cultural consequences. Given the historical closeness of the fields, the failure to observe disciplinary borders exacerbates, rather than ameliorates, competitive and even exploitative relations between them. Inevitably, territorial skirmishes have developed as psychology expressed antagonism toward religion and religionists ignored or depreciated psychological ideas.

Since the early 1980s, American cultural conditions favorable to religion have fostered a rapprochement between the disciplines of psychology and theology that has only slightly solved the disciplinary confusion problem. These cultural conditions are twofold: the entrenched popularity of psychology and the renewed popularity of religions of all brands, including the most zealous and radical forms. The result has been each discipline's grudging, superficial, and fragile acknowledgment of the other's rightful domain rather than, as earlier, a type of plagiaristic appropriating and redefining of concepts and terms from one realm of discourse to fit them into the other. This mutual acknowledgment, limited though it may be, is a welcome development.

Next, we should examine an interesting and popular amalgam of psychology and religious creed that has become known by the term *spiritual healing*, which includes healing of both physical and emotional disorders by spiritual methods (Evans 1989). That God can and does heal has been believed by religious people almost universally. Spiritual healing, however, does not merely refer to this belief but also to a set of assumptions about the specific ways positive change takes place in the lives of disturbed individuals. An examination of the diverse spiritual healing literature suggests that the targets of healing include the whole range of emotional and cognitive disorders that already had been carefully defined and differentiated through psychological research into mental disorders. The modern spiritual healing writers heavily borrow conceptual terminology from psychological research literature with minimal acknowledgment, probably because they are not much aware of their debt to psychology.

In the case of religious healing of physical disease, there is not much danger of spiritual healers mimicking medical methods or concepts. Such an effort would seem clearly bogus—for example, if a spiritual healer gave out spiritual pills or performed a spiritual brand of surgery. The normally physical modes (palpation, pharmacology, surgery, etc.) used by medical personnel are in clear contrast to the verbal, cognitive, interpersonal, and experiential modes by which spiritual power is believed to be brought to bear on a disease. These latter methods are the ancient and venerable stock in trade of the religious community.

In contrast, there is considerable danger of spiritual healers adapting psychotherapy methods and concepts so that they fit within a given theological framework. This adaptation includes, but is not limited to, interpretation of unconscious processes, relaxation and stress control techniques, and cognitive restructuring methods. In fact, its widespread occurrence with little or no acknowledgment of source should be a matter of some embarrassment to religious people of integrity. This confusion is partly the fault of psychologists who have been loathe to define the borders of their discipline, having instead unwisely preferred them to remain a highly permeable membrane.

With widespread popular interest in both religion and psychology, it has been easy for some religious writers and teachers to convince their readers and followers that their own psychological spins are novel and have grown directly from deep religious insight and/or divine revelation. Successful misrepresentation has depended heavily on the psychological ignorance of their followers. In a similar way, some psychological writers have exploited the renewed interest in religious issues to imply that religious truth can be construed as flowing merely from a careful consideration of basic psychological principles. Both of these exploitations are most unfortunate.

This appropriation of ideas by well-informed writers and teachers may be an attempt at religious outreach, appealing to the public desire for a simplistic integration of two important but disparate realms of discourse. Or it may be for personal aggrandizement and financial gain. Often it is a pragmatic strategy designed to promote the benefits of one's own field, either religion or psychology, by identifying closely with the most attractive and popular features of the other. Again, both psychologists and religious leaders have been guilty of these exploitations.

AN EXAMPLE OF APPROPRIATED CONCEPTS: SELF-ESTEEM

The powerful psychological concept of self-esteem, theoretically and empirically supported by dozens of thoughtful and well-designed studies (e.g., Taylor 1989), has been mistakenly claimed by various religious writers and speakers as inherently religious. In their view, psychology is understood as having simply happened upon a preexisting set of insights embedded within religious beliefs and tradition. An example of this line of reasoning is that the moral imperative of doing unto others what you would want done to you implies the presupposition that you love and care for yourself enough that you would want good done to you. Thus, the concept of self-esteem is purported to be essentially and historically a religious idea stemming from a religious imperative.

It can be meaningfully argued that *all* ideas are originally religious. Discoveries in archeology, new theories in physics, philosophical methods, mathematical strategies—all can be considered to have originated with God and therefore within theology. In historical practice, however, it has not happened that way. Although theology has a well-developed subfield called "anthropology" (not to be confused with the social science of that name) that theorizes about human nature in its relationship to God and the spiritual domain, the modern carefully delineated idea of self-esteem does not appear as such in its literature (e.g., Berkouwer 1962). Ironically, the concept most closely related to it is the human propensity for pride— to think *more highly* of yourself than you should, leading to rebellion against God. Thus, self-esteem, as theology sees it, has traditionally been considered a potentially dangerous temptation.

That the psychological idea of self-esteem, deriving from the psychoanalytic and self-theorists' literature, should be appropriated by popular religion, is one of the most ironic of recent intellectual developments. For example, Robert Schuller, well-known pastor of the Garden Grove Crystal Cathedral near Los Angeles, argues that the primeval fall of humankind is not primarily a fall involving sinful rebelliousness, but rather a disastrous loss of self-esteem that has subsequently undercut human happiness and effective living (Schuller 1982). Schuller not only incorporates a peculiarly psychological concept into his creedal structure; he makes it a centerpiece.

Although it cannot be denied that there are parallel ideas, and implications of ideas, to be found across disciplines, ascribing the concept of self-esteem to religion is mistaken and confusing. It is analogous to claiming that basic principles of modern dermatology are found in the Levitical priestly code concerning ritual uncleanness. There is ample evidence that the idea of self-esteem has been developed within psychology as a corollary of several theories, including psychoanalysis, self theory, Gestalt theory, existential theory, and several discrete forms of personality theory (Taylor 1989). Suggestions that the presence of embryonic elements of the concept of self-esteem in religious literature shows that literature to be the source of the ideas imply a retrogressive confusion of two spheres of discourse, one of which is currently in the delicate process of self-definition.

Examined closely, the *self* concept does not qualify as a spiritual idea that applies to human spirit; rather it applies to human mind. This distinction arises repeatedly in this book as we consider in depth the disciplinary boundaries of psychology and its cognate fields. A spirit-relevant concept pertains to a putative domain of spirits and a human's participation in it. The existence of this spiritual, sometimes called *metaphysical*, domain has been generally assumed throughout most of human history, until the Enlightenment in Europe when religious skepticism became more popular among the middle and aristocratic classes and the secularization of Western culture accelerated.

For some, a nearly automatic modern reaction to the mention of spirit, or even mind, is that these ideas seem to be obviously untenable. When considered truly philosophically, however, the category of the physical *(phisikos)* is no more or less respectable than the categories of mind and spirit (Rychlak 1993). It is only because of the strongly materialistic bias of modern Western thought that science is inclined to deem bodily considerations more fundamental than others.[7] Currently there is a somewhat regressive borrowing of credibility and authority, with religion tending to borrow from psychology and psychology tending to borrow from biology/medicine as each discipline tries to enhance its own standing in the modern intellectual milieu.

This continued diminishing of cultural belief in a spiritual domain—sometimes identified also with postmodernism—has led to a reactive effort by some to salvage and rehabilitate a number of its previously most cherished and meaningful ideas, ideas that have played important parts in the emotional lives of many people. By analogy, consider how difficult it is to discontinue celebrating a religious holiday even after beliefs surrounding the holiday are no longer held. A romantic attachment to these ideas among those who grew up with them but who, as adults, found them untenable sometimes motivates this nostalgic search for comforts from the past.

With psychology developing almost simultaneously with religion's accelerated decline in the West, the new field became a primary source for borrowing by religionists. Especially mined were those ideas within psychology that are consistent with the personhood inherent in most spiritual ideologies. The notion of a self-concept was a natural candidate for such borrowing. When it became clear that it was difficult for modern religious writers and teachers to credibly teach the existence of a personal soul or spirit, they sometimes gravitated toward certain psychological theorists, such as Gordon Allport, Abraham Maslow, Carl Rogers, and those in the self-theory psychoanalytic tradition, who had at least preserved a belief in human personhood (versus a mechanical or animal model of personality). In this sense, psychology provided an important transitional service for certain religious teachers until they could redefine and reestablish the credibility of their own sphere of discourse.

To some extent the 1980s and 1990s have seen a revitalization of interest and belief in the spiritual sphere with the advent of the New Age movement and the worldwide resurgence of traditional religious systems of all varieties. As psychology's cognitive revolution ushered in a refined form of mentalism, religion more easily made a credible case for spiritual realities. I would assert that completing this task must include a careful differentiation of spiritual from psychological concepts—a differentiation some are loath to undertake for fear of diminishing religion's prestige.

Two examples illustrate the borrowing of psychological concepts by religious writers and teachers. The first is the concept of emotional security, developed by Karen Horney (1937) and others in the psychoanalytic tradition in the 1930s. Feeling emotionally safe as a consequence of growing up in a nonthreatening emotional environment—Horney's idea—was quickly seen as an idea that could be sculpted to fit spiritual teaching purposes. Sermons, books, pamphlets, and newspaper articles by religious writers and clergy asserted then and now the equivalence of spiritual peace—what in a former era might have been called a "state of grace"—with a psychological condition of inner security. But the two concepts are by no means synonymous. Emotional *security* may obtain when a person is not in a healthy spiritual state, and emotional *insecurity* may obtain when a person is in a healthy spiritual state. The ideas are from different realms of discourse and the semantic relations between them are very complex. Confusion will inevitably result from treating the psychological concept of security as equivalent to the theological concept of grace.

The second example has to do with anger. For centuries, religionists had warned people of the moral dangers related to anger. Now adept at borrowing, the religious community has incorporated psychology's ideas about dealing with anger. Training people to be more cognizant of their anger, and more skilled in channeling, expressing, and restraining it, is an important cultural contribution of psychoanalysis and psychotherapeutics. Learning ways to acknowledge and incorporate anger into one's self-concept, and to deal with it in a more effective, detached, and morally neutral manner, were clearly the innovations of psychological theorists.

These methods for handling anger became widespread topics of religious discourse, and sometimes this led to a level of excusing morally reprehensible behavior and attitudes that is inappropriate within religion's sphere. Although it is thought appropriate, even essential, for psychological theorists and therapists temporarily to regard morally objectionable behavior (e.g., criminal, offensive, aggressive, or inappropriate sexual behavior) as morally neutral, in general it is neither functional nor appropriate for those representing moral/religious leadership to do so. The same can be said of the judicial/penal system. The *psychological* effort to understand how personal agency works requires that moral issues be set aside for the moment in favor of the specific goal of understanding and changing a given behavior. But it is a mistake to attempt moral neutrality in the spiritual sphere. Although some social critics have held behavioral science responsible for lowering society's moral standards, it is more correct to say that behavioral science concepts and methods have been used inappropriately in spheres of discourse for which they were not intended.

It is interesting to credit a few who have noticed and objected to this violation of disciplinary boundaries. Within popular culture, the song "Officer Krupke" from the movie of the Broadway musical *West Side Story* offers a parody on this attitude as early as the 1950s, providing an example of a growing social reaction.[8] The attitudes of social scientists dealing with delinquent urban gang youth in the musical are shown as abrogating moral authority on the grounds that the behavior is explicable in terms of poverty, prejudice, and educational disadvantage. Those who watched the musical instantly understood the point being made.[9]

It is difficult to document the inception of this borrowing of psychological concepts by the religious community, or even to date its origin accurately, because of the widespread inclusion in the United States of psychological ideas in some religious writing as early as the 1920s and 1930s. In those decades few raised their voices against the practice. Psychologists were pleased to have popular recognition for their fledgling ideas, and theologians/pastors were relieved to have something to fill the confessional void caused by a growing modern and postmodern religious skepticism.

A pioneer in this practice was Mary Baker Eddy (1821–1910), who founded the Christian Science Church in 1879. Eddy clearly stands within the New Thought psychological tradition that played such an important part in the early formation of popular psychology (Meyer 1980). This tradition taught the primacy of mind over matter and so held to the existence of mind at the very time the concept of mind was gradually losing credibility among psychologists and other academics. Later, Norman Vincent Peale, pastor of Manhattan's Marble Collegiate Church for several decades, was enormously influential in spreading the "gospel" of the power of positive thinking (mind) as a quasi-religious teaching (*The Power of Positive Thinking*, 1953). Robert Schuller (1982) continues promulgating the same idea.

These, then, are examples of the inappropriate use of mental concepts from psychology's sphere of discourse, showing how the concepts have served a credibility-enhancing function for religious individuals and institutions. And though this is not the place to document the weaker converse phenomenon, it is also true that certain moral and religious ideas have been intermittently used, especially within the past decade or so, to give authority and prestige to some goals of certain portions of the psychological community without adequate recognition of their value-laden and nonempirical nature. Suffice it to say that this confounding of religious and psychological ideas continues unabated, with small recognition of epistemic issues that properly separate the two spheres of discourse.

KEY TRANSITIONAL FIGURES

Carl Rogers (1967) provides an illuminating example of the drift from one sphere of discourse to another. In fact, he was a pioneer in appropriating certain religious ideas into psychology and a psychologist who tacitly encouraged the religious community to employ psychological ideas.

In his youth Rogers intended to pursue a career in Christian ministry. Following college graduation he enrolled at Union Theological Seminary in New York. Through exposure to psychology in one of his pastoral training courses, he became interested in clinical psychology and eventually transferred into Columbia University's Teacher's College, where he completed a Ph.D. in psychology (Hilgard 1987).

Rogers (1967) documents his growing difficulty in accepting traditional spiritual categories and beliefs. He identifies a connection between the shrinking strength of his theological creed and his growing interest in psychology's potential for human benefit. An almost conscious substitution of psychological for theological ideas took place, with the flagship substitution of his well-known concept of unconditional positive regard for the central Christian idea of utter forgiveness and reconciliation of the sinner—an idea with which Rogers grew up in a devout household.

An examination of Rogers's personality theory and therapy approach in *On Becoming a Person* (1961), for example, reveals many of the values and attitudes toward life and existence traditionally found in a Christian world view *minus* the metaphysical or transcendent dimension. Deep respect for the value of the person underlies much of what Rogers says about the relationship between client and therapist, but he fails to disclose why he believes the person ought to be valued or why valuing the person should play such an important role in therapy.

The theological underpinnings for these ideas were present in his childhood and adolescent religious instruction, and many of his avid followers shared a personal history of religious heritage. The presuppositional nature of his ideas is more or less ignored in Rogers's presentation of his view of personality and the nature of the therapy process—an oversight that would be unlikely in today's atmosphere of heightened awareness of value issues in science.

In truth, every theory and practice of psychology, like Rogers's, is set in a context of values, and their evaluators now are freer to accept or reject them according to the degree of compatibility between their own values and those of the theorists being considered. But at the time Rogers wrote, the myth of value-neutrality prevailing among his readership obscured the absence of an adequate justification for the strong values he asserted within the fabric of his personality theory.

Rogers was rather careful to define his borrowed ideas in an appropriately psychological way (i.e., as applying to mind or agency), but the initial religious framework of the origins of these ideas was transparent to many. In this awareness, religious writers, teachers, and clergy then translated back ideas that Rogers had cast in a psychological framework. Because the ideas' affinity with theological concepts was apparent, it was a small step to rebaptize them into a theological status. Thus, for example, unconditional positive regard, as defined within therapeutic psychology, became identical in much religious writing and teaching with the grace of God as revealed in Scripture.

OTHER TRANSITIONAL FIGURES

The book *I And Thou* by Jewish philosopher/theologian Martin Buber (1958), important in shaping theology for the 1960s, provides another example of the profound psychologizing of theology in which the focus has been shifted from primarily metaphysical concerns to relational ones (i.e., putting relationship at the core of the concept of God). Certainly the transcendent dimension is not omitted, but the emphasis has shifted to a deep absorption with the topic of the nature of personal knowing and how it occurs. It is a psychological question at its core.

The same psychological themes are apparent in the writings of Paul Tillich, preeminent among twentieth-century existential theologians. His emphasis on the human search for meaning illustrates twentieth-century attempts to discover a ground for permanent values in human experience. Using what are essentially psychological methods, Tillich tries to establish truth that transcends the human personality. His titanic intellectual accomplishment of making religion meaningful to thousands of mid-twentieth-century seekers set the course for countless preachers, teachers, and theorists who also translated psychological terms into religious language. But this trend has led to enormous confusion and has made it difficult for a layperson considering a particular article of religious belief to identify its epistemic core as either religious or scientific/psychological.

Tillich's semiautobiographical description of the way he began to reformulate his theological method is aptly titled *The Shaking of the Foundations* (1948). In it, he identifies the problem he faced as one who could no longer believe the factual basis of Christianity as literal truth. His task was to make the Christian story phenomenologically (subjectively) meaningful—in effect, to psychologize it. This endeavor led to further confusion of the disciplinary boundaries—theological truth and psychological truth became indistinguishable.

In the late 1970s, the massive popular assent to disciplinary confusion took place through such key figures as M. Scott Peck. A Harvard-trained psychiatrist, Peck brought to his lecturing seminars impeccable credentials and excellent communication skills. His best-selling books, *The Road Less Traveled* (1979) and *People of the Lie* (1983), are fascinating amalgams of religious beliefs, most of them loosely derived from the Judaic-Christian tradition, with interpersonal principles deriving from social and personality/clinical research. *The Road Less Traveled* is subtitled "A New Psychology of Love, Traditional Values, and Spiritual Growth." Peck's willingness to take a strong moral stance obviously appeals to an enormous readership who sense a serious breakdown of moral thinking and behavior in our time. Within the smaller but growing evangelical Christian community, psychologist James Dobson (1974) performs much the same role as does Peck. In these popular writers, both of whom have excellent academic training, there is a curious failure to carefully distinguish psychologically based assertions from religious and value assertions, a relaxation of discipline boundaries that are important in separating religion and psychology.

Pastoral Counseling

In thinking about the problem of blurred disciplinary lines, we should also consider the well-established field of pastoral counseling. A pastoral counselor, who usually holds a theological degree and has taken additional training in psychology, focuses his or her professional attention on faith-oriented people who bring problems that are typically, but not always, faith related in some way. In this way, a pastoral counselor could be compared to a psychologist who only takes patients with eating disorders. The pastoral counselor often deals with many of the same disorders seen in any psychological clinic, including relational and family problems. The difference rests with the clients; they come from a particular population that functions within a restricted creedal boundary.

If a pastoral counselor is also functioning in capacities other than counseling and has not been fully trained in the specialty area of pastoral counseling, he or she usually is quick to acknowledge that limitation by referring clients who manifest disorders that are beyond the pastoral counselor's treatment competency to other professionals. When established psychological counseling principles are appropriately applied to religious believers or to ministry-related problems, pastoral psychology does *not* contribute to blurred disciplines.

By way of example, I will return to the topic of guilt. A well-trained pastoral counselor is careful not to confuse the subjective sense of guilt with ontological guilt, theologically defined. In the same way, God's existence will not be reduced to the equivalent of that which a person most values or any other psychological phenomenon. For these reasons and from experience in my own practice, I believe pastoral counseling is not a prime offender in the disciplinary confusions about which we are thinking.

PROPER SEPARATION

Having identified some issues and some prominent personalities that illustrate the unfortunate blurring of boundaries between religion and psychology, what can I say on the positive, constructive side to offer guidelines for the relationship between disciplines that maintain the autonomy of each while encouraging the kind of cross-boundary dialogue that is ultimately beneficial to both?

By far the most typical response to that query is to focus on the methodological differences between the disciplines; that is, to reaffirm that while religion bases its beliefs on faith and unprovable assumptions, psychology purports to be scientific and thus bases its beliefs on demonstrable and replicable facts discoverable through empirical research. While this differentiation is partly defensible, current philosophy of science persuasively calls into question this neat distinction as a way to differentiate between types of disciplines. (Polanyi 1958)

Today we are much more aware that most science, and surely psychology is primary here, rests on a whole range of unprovable assumptions concerning the nature of reality and how it is investigated. Similarly, many sincere religionists believe that their beliefs rest on historical events combined with reasonable interpretations of those events and are, therefore, neither epistemically arbitrary—so-called leaps of faith—nor empirically foundationless. So method by itself is not the answer.

If the methodological distinction alone does not hold, is there another basis on which a meaningful distinction between psychology and religion can be maintained? If psychology is not to be readily assimilated into spirituality, or if psychology is not to try to assimilate religion into itself, some other definitional guidelines must be specified and consensually acknowledged.

And so we return to the main theme of this book. From its beginning psychology's focus was the mind, the personal agent of choice.[10] In mind there is the recognition of personal identity, of significant consciousness, of what Joseph Rychlak (1988) alternatively calls "logos." *Mind* pertains to how persons purposefully shape their lives or fail to do so, how they look after and actualize their abilities and potentialities. The laws or principles by which psychological science proceeds need not rest on any particular metaphysical view of the nature of things different from other empirical sciences—with the one important exception that it does affirm the existence of *mind*. That affirmation is the thread that runs through all its pursuits and gives it a distinctive identity.

Does accepting mind as the focus of psychology commit one to a particular worldview, as some fear? While some contend that this affirmation inescapably implies a cosmos that is essentially personal rather than impersonal, or even implies some form of theism, others do not come to this conclusion. Rather, they contend that the evolutionary process may well have led to human personality without consciousness necessarily having originated from a cosmic personal consciousness.[11] While this latter view of personal consciousness may tend to depreciate the ultimate value of human life (some would say trivialize its value), it is at least conceivable that personal consciousness has arisen from an impersonal cosmos. This seems to be, in fact, the position taken by astrophysicist Stephen Hawking (1993).

Other thinkers reason that a stream cannot rise higher than its source; therefore, if personality or agency truly exists in humankind, it reflects a personal cosmos. This happens to be my own view. However, in either view, psychology needs to affirm the existence of mind, that is, the genuine agency and primacy of consciousness in the individual, but as a discipline it need not further specify the nature of reality. At minimum the metaphysic must allow the notion of mind and its knowability. Beyond this, it can accommodate a wide range of viewpoints.

PSYCHOLOGY AND MORAL VALUES

A psychology with mind at the center is not necessarily quasi-religious. In contrast to religion, psychology as a scientific discipline does not assume a moral stance. Presupposing mind to be the rather narrow focus of psychology's study does not require psychology to take moral positions in the usual sense. It only requires the consistent recognition of each person's central organizing agency on which psychological research and theory is focused.

Recognizing mind has sometimes been mistaken for taking a moral stance, as might be true of recognizing spirit. It is, rather, a *philosophical* stance. Psychology embodies values that are broadly scientific in character, as does any science (e.g., promoting the growth of empirically based, meaningful knowledge), but those values do not necessarily include altruism or prosocial concern. On this point, it is important to make a distinction between psychologists as persons and the essential discipline of psychology. Although individual psychologists or even political/social organizations of psychologists, such as the American Psychological Association, may adhere to certain key prosocial, ethical, or moral principles, those principles should not be assumed to be inherent in the discipline itself. All of these facts considered, psychology is firmly within the scientific tradition. In this sense, psychology stands in relation to society exactly as does, for example, biology. Surveillance of science in general, and of psychology in particular, to make certain that its overall influence is prosocial will always be important to the societies in which psychologists work. Ombudsmen mediating between society's interests and psychology's search for knowledge perform a valuable function, and they have become prominent toward the end of the twentieth century. For example, they take the form of committees and officials in the American Psychological Association and the American Psychological Society responsible for developing acceptable ethical guidelines.

Still, in principle these ombudsmen stand just outside the discipline, negotiating with the broader society for the needed freedom to investigate aspects of mind whose investigation might otherwise be considered socially unacceptable. Thus Freud's exploration of infantile sexuality and of unconscious processes met with intense resistance when they were first disclosed. To fulfill its mandate, psychology must function within socially acceptable ethical boundaries and sometimes must negotiate with society for the freedom to do so. This is equally true for physicists and biologists.

What advantage is there to a discipline that studies *mind* but carefully avoids specific moral stances on important social issues? The answer is that eleven decades of psychological research, while following that path to a limited degree, have yielded valuable fruit on fundamental psychological questions that they might otherwise not have produced. In the 1990s we have seen psychology's increased willingness to comply with various ethical guidelines, especially in the delivery of psychological services, but it has been slower to show integrity in resuming its focus of inquiry into mind as its designated special domain. Reclaiming its special mandate is its next large task.

PSYCHOLOGY AND THE SUPERNATURAL

Psychology differentiates from religion not only in refraining from a moral stance but also in taking no position on the existence of a world of spiritual beings or a personal transcendent realm. Again it is good to remind ourselves of the postmodern insight of Polanyi, Kuhn, and other philosophers of science that some view of reality stands behind all scientific theorizing and experimenting. But psychology is free to declare itself independent of, and neutral with respect to, the spiritual transcendent position held by many religions (i.e., the existence of personal being(s) not perceptible to the physical senses).

Although I, on separate and independent grounds, affirm a belief in metaphysical reality, I also believe that psychology must remain neutral relative to any such view. Even though such a neutral posture is not popular in the late 1990s, it is important for the future of our discipline because it allows for contributions by people who hold a wide range of viewpoints concerning a putative supernatural realm.

It is important to remember that psychology's focus on mind does not exclude subconscious or nonconscious mental processes. The affirmation of subconscious or nonconscious processes has sometimes been mistaken for belief in a supernatural realm on the grounds that subconscious processes in some way reflect a spiritual dimension. Freud (1927) held that a strong concept of subconscious can be maintained in the absence of an espoused theology. Carl Jung (1916), on the other hand, deliberately linked the unconscious to sources of spirituality, thereby proposing a bridge between the two putative realms of reality.

Freud grounded his view of the unconscious on a materialist base—a superfluous and misleading foundation because it added nothing to his idea. And the Jungian link between the unconscious and spirituality was likewise a mistake that has damaged psychology as an empirical discipline because it gave the mistaken impression that an essential and irreplaceable link exists between a rigorously empirical psychology of mind and a quasi-religious stance of some type.

It is imperative that psychology not try to become a new secular priesthood (Vitz 1977) and not confound itself with religious doctrine of any kind. It must become aware of its own distinctive place in the array of human studies and understand that that place centers on its bold and consistent presupposition of the existence of mind. That presupposition is its raison d'etre. The development of a consensus by psychologists on this issue is critical.

Disciplines need strong identities before they attempt any cross-disciplinary blend. But historically, with its youthful sense of invincibility, psychology has not observed this restraint. It has prematurely joined itself to movements and disciplines, some religious, on the basis of expediency rather than identity-shaped principles.

With the renewed interest in religion in the 1990s represented by the growth of movements such as New Age, fundamentalist Christianity, spiritual healing, and positive thinking, strong pressure to blend a religious worldview with psychology has diffused psychology's public image. Almost any self-appointed spokesperson can be accepted as representing psychology, and the discipline has lost most of its authority to publicly dissociate itself from such spokespersons even when they take positions that have little to do with psychology.

At issue here is not whether it is appropriate that there are Psychologists Interested in Religious Issues (the title assumed by a fairly new American Psychological Association division), because psychologists can take legitimate interest in any number of culture's facets. Rather the fundamental issue is whether an entire discipline that affirms mind can do so without also affirming spirit. In a culture, and within a language tradition, that has not consistently differentiated between mind and spirit, the maturing of such a discipline requires vigilant, deliberate, and focused effort.

NOTES

1. Paul Vitz (1977) has written in detail about the pervasive tendency in some circles for psychologists to take over the functions of traditional clergy and for clergy to imitate psychologists at the expense of their spiritual functions. He ascribes this trend to the simultaneous cultural decline of ecclesiastical and spiritual authority and the ascendency of psychology.

2. Another way to ask this question is to wonder whether the reductionist is of the eliminative sort, that is, inclined to eliminate the higher order discipline as superfluous. It is possible to believe that all information about a discipline is somehow contained within another, more basic, discipline (e.g., biology within chemistry) without considering the derivative, higher order discipline to be redundant or even likely to be redundant someday. Instead, it is simply recognized that the new discipline contains indispensable categories and concepts. Thus, one who holds such a belief is not an eliminative reductionist. It seems to me, however, that for most nonphilosophers, including psychologists, there is a fairly strong tendency for a benign reductionism to devolve into an eliminative type, especially under any pressure of professional rivalry such as currently exists in the mental health professions.

3. Many Christian believers no longer hold to even a mind and body dualism, on the grounds that such a teaching is an import into the New Testament from Greek philosophy, and therefore a corruption, and that the Old Testament consistently teaches a mind-body monism. In this view, the soul, or spirit, or mind (synonymous terms in their view) is simply a way to describe the "personality" or "self" system of the person and should not be reified to have the same status as the body. However, Ann and Barry Ulanov (1975) cogently point out that

the soul is harder . . . to locate and in an age of scientism particularly difficult to define. That does not for a moment persuade those who have met the soul in their work in depth psychology, or religion . . . that the soul is simply a remnant of a looser time in human intellectual enterprise or a continuing mark of superstition or easy credulity, sooner or later to be replaced by the discoveries and determinations of more tough-minded scientists. Unquestionably, the word has been used awkwardly, inexactly. . . . Nonetheless, "soul" describes very well, with a rich tradition of experience as well as speculation behind it, the organizing principle of life, that which the body gives up when it turns from a living organism into a cadaver. (82)

4. In chapter 5, I will point out the significant contribution Peck has made to psychology's identity search.

5. For example, if a psychologist were working with someone who had committed a crime against another while in a rage, it might be important to reduce debilitating guilt feelings to avoid suicidal behaviors. The ontological guilt, however, is completely untouched by this process.

6. In his personal search for absolutes, Tillich (1967) was able to identify the following as absolute:

the structure of the mind that makes sense impressions possible, and the logical and semantic structure of the mind; the universals that make language possible; the categories and polarities that make understanding reality possible. Others [are] the unconditional character of the moral imperative, regardless of its contents, and the principle of justice—acknowledgment of every person as a person. Finally, there [is] *agape*, love, which contains and transcends justice and unites the absolute and the relative by adapting itself to every concrete situation . . . . we found something else . . . that all the absolutes pointed beyond themselves to the most basic absolute of all, to being-itself beyond the split of subject and object. (124)

7. I am speaking here of eliminative reductionist materialism to which I believe many intellectuals and nonintellectuals are prone. Professional philosophers are probably the exceptions.

8. Ernest Lehmen based his screenplay of *West Side Story* on the book by Arthur Laurents.

9. Karl Menninger (1988) also raises the question as the title of his best-selling book, *Whatever Became of Sin?* He clearly saw that the idea of moral culpability was in need of rehabilitation. His was one of a number of voices expressing the harmful impact they believed a pervasive acceptance of a social science perspective was having on society, not simply in the limited setting of a psychiatric or psychological consultation but from the pulpit and in the pastor's study as well.

10. *Mind* is simply the most natural and oldest designation for the focus of psychological science. But clustered around it are related concepts that also connote personal agency and warm, human, unique individual presence. Some of these concepts are *self*, *logos*, and *consciousness*.

11. This idea is related to "emergentism" in a reductionist position, where it is held that something *qualitatively* new and superior can arise out of a more basic framework of understanding.

3
Psychology in Contrast with Medicine

*T*here is another socially powerful academic and applied discipline that threatens to make psychology a derivative of itself: medicine. The so-called medical model of psychological dysfunction has been an important source of controversy in psychology for several decades (Szasz 1970). Historically, psychologists have more readily acknowledged the threat of medicine rather than religion as a potential trespasser into the rightful domain of psychology. This difference likely arises from the increasing prestige and social leverage that medicine has been able to accrue simultaneously with the waning influence of religion during the first part of the twentieth century.[1]

Medicine has repeatedly asserted its inherent privilege to direct and control therapeutic processes, especially in the delivery of services, including treatment of various levels of mental problems. It claims a mandate as society's primary healing profession. Since the 1700s in the Western world medicine has gradually won the healing role that the Christian priesthood had held as the principal practitioner of physical and spiritual healing during the Middle Ages. The rise of the modern biosciences prompted this primacy in healing to be accorded medicine, a primacy that it has held ever since.

The authoritarian form of organization quite naturally prevailed in medicine because of the era of its origin, and this authoritarianism, combined with the great prestige of natural science, resulted in unprecedented power, wealth, and prestige for the physician. Other workers in the healing enterprise, including nurses, technicians, physical therapists, and administrators, were regarded as adjunctive and supplementary, playing their part in a course of treatment assumed to be best orchestrated by the physician.

Medicine today maintains its social power by training cadre after cadre of well-qualified professionals. Medical students—potential physicians—are carefully selected for native intelligence, great diligence, and generally compassionate attitudes toward sufferers. They are well trained and deeply imbued with healthy scientific skepticism together with the need to rely in their work, if at all possible, on experimentally proven findings. All of these qualities serve to perpetuate medicine's authority.

It is not surprising that in the first decades of the twentieth century the social responsibility for remedying or ameliorating mental disorders was given to medical doctors. No other profession had more information about mental disorders (although it could be argued that lawyers, clergy, and teachers at the time had as much), and physicians were known as diligent, skeptical scientists, well equipped for this difficult task.

When the term illness was first used to designate mental problems, it was a step forward over the simplistic moralism that blamed the sufferer for the symptom. But because the effect was to move the problem from the spiritual domain (judging disordered behavior according to some moral standard) to the physical domain (that of sickness), the task was only half complete. The domain of the mind was not yet clearly established in the public consciousness. It still is not. Instead, mental illness as simply another form of medical disease gradually became part of the vernacular, a knee-jerk way to think about mental disorders.

The pervasive triumph of this close linking of medicine and mental dysfunction is nowhere more clearly expressed than in the current enlightened pronouncements of journalists, commentators, and public service ads stressing *mental illness* as an important issue for social consciousness raising. What is not as widely recognized by such spokespersons is that labeling mental problems as *illness* prejudges them as falling within the physical and medical domain of investigation and knowledge. Every such media piece both expresses and reinforces the connection.

That a problem exists with the dominance of medicine in helping those who are mentally disturbed flows reasonably from my theme: There is a separate domain of human functioning that is *neither* spiritual nor physical. Let us examine this idea a bit more.

AN OBJECTION: THE MISTAKE OF REIFYING MIND

"To reify is to invent a concept, give it a name, and then convince ourselves that such a thing objectively exists in the world" (Myers 1995, 370). Accordingly, it could be pointed out that *mind* is not a fixed and objectively real thing, and that to treat it as such is to view an abstract concept (mind) as if it were real and concrete.

This objection is valid if we assume that what is real or *most* real is what is tangible, concrete, and perceptible by everyone—in a word, *material*. It is almost second nature for us to believe that only matter is significant, that "material" and "actual" are synonyms. These beliefs are at the core of philosophical materialism. Although few psychologists would pronounce themselves consistent materialists, they decry reifying any concept that is not matter. I strongly believe this is a mistake.

Some thoughtful philosophers of science point out that matter itself has been reified—it has been ascribed the status of normative reality.[2] There is nothing intrinsic to matter that makes it *more real* than anything else in the universe unless one takes the preeminent reality status of matter as simply axiomatic. Religionists typically add at least one more category of reality to that of matter—spiritual reality. This book proposes that psychology at its best has always added a third category, *mind*, and that the pioneers of psychology as a discipline generally operated in relation to that category.

Professionals who believe in and are instructed concerning the realm of spirit beings (priests, ministers, rabbis, shamans, and other clerics) are presumably best qualified to instruct and treat people in relation to this spiritual realm. Professionals trained in anatomy, physiology, organ pathology, and clinical therapeutics (physicians and other bioclinicians) are presumably best qualified to instruct and treat people in the physical realm. But what about the domain of the mind, that area of human functioning that is neither *primarily* spiritual nor *primarily* physical?

Does such a domain exist? According to popular Western philosophical materialism, thinking and learning, emotional life, religious belief, and interpersonal relationships come down to the movements of atoms, molecules, tissues, and organs with their various changes in form. In addition to that pervasive, culture-wide conviction, a subset of society believes in a spirit realm that supplements the physical realm. These two views (i.e., pure materialism and materialism laced with some form of spiritual reality) account for the contemporary majority perspective in Western society. Relatively few people include in their worldview what I am proposing in this book, a third discrete category of human functioning, a domain of the *mind*, which includes human causal agency and conscious selfhood that is distinct from the domains of both body and spirit. The traditional dualist view of human functioning has been difficult to challenge. The vested interests of the clerical and medical professions significantly slow the pace of change.

Serious public advocates of the third sphere that is neither physical nor spiritual have typically included those who have personally benefited from psychotherapy. They often state their conviction that they had previously exhausted the resources of both medical and spiritual expertise without relief. Their intractable personal problems or life questions have yielded only to a specifically psychological solution (e.g., Beers 1908).

FREUD'S ROLE AS A PIONEER OF MENTALISM

In chapter 1 I pointed out the irony of a physician, Sigmund Freud, making the first major contribution to psychology. Freud's theory, loosely set in a materialist matrix of constructs, does not depend for its value or its validity on that matrix (Rychlak 1993). It has been said correctly that Freud just as easily could have been an attorney or a cleric without essentially altering the core of his theory. His psychoanalytic theory does not depend upon the particular closed materialist philosophy to which Freud subscribed.

His theory loudly proclaims psychological theorizing autonomous from theology and medicine. He was disdainful of religion, so that part was easy for him. But, more surprising, he believed that psychoanalysts need not be trained in medicine—a view that his more territorially minded followers chose to ignore. When doctorally trained nonmedical individuals applied for psychoanalytic training in the early part of the twentieth century, they were denied that training in direct contradiction to Freud's own instruction (Cohen 1992).[3] The truth is that Freud saw his seminal ideas as locating naturally neither within religion nor within medicine, but launching out into the truly new territory of the mental. His generation accurately dubbed his work "the new psychology."

Although Freud may have derived some heuristic benefit from the concurrently developing laws of thermodynamics and from ideas of changes in forms of energy within a physical system, his idea of the moving libido in normal child development was essentially a mental, not a physical, phenomenon (Rychlak 1993). Similarly, although the id is an expression of biological survival need in the individual, and thus its bodily basis is duly set forth (satisfying Freud's own materialist bias), its further early life development into ego and superego does not reasonably require reference to any *physical* concomitants to be fully understood. This was an essential insight of the neo-Freudians, who asserted that the ego is its own energy source and is not perpetually dependent for energy on the id (which is conceived as body based).

Despite the fact that Freud's crucial idea of the unconscious implies that much of human behavior has purpose best understood in terms of evolutionary survival rather than deliberate conscious intention, the unconscious as a repository of memories and a master control of behavior is a thoroughly mentalist idea that need not rest on biological assumptions. That Freud tied them to biology is simply an historical accident. The biological framework is an optional way to construe the unconscious.[4]

Few conceptions of mind have rivaled the prototypic and iconic clarity of Freud's visions of the id, ego, superego, conscious, preconscious, and subconscious. Those who take Freud's ideas seriously today can do so because they understand them to be models of psychological reality, thereby partially demythologizing them. Others, by contrast, construe Freud, in his relatively naive philosophy of science, as having mistakenly reified his constructs. This may or may not be true. What is important for our purposes is that the objective reality of mind is so consistently assumed in Freud's theory that iconic descriptions of its putative anatomy and physiology, such as superego and id, seemed perfectly appropriate to him. This also should be true for us, even if we discard his particular descriptions.

THE MENTALISM OF OTHER EARLY PSYCHOLOGISTS

Carving out a special place for a science of the mind as distinct from spiritual or physical reality was clearly the intent of other early psychologists. While Gustaf Fechner (1860) was trained as a neurophysiological scientist, his writings indicate his desire to initiate a science that mediates between soul and body. Especially in his later writings that attempt to show the link between mind and matter, between what he called inner psychophysics and outer psychophysics, Fechner believed he was founding a new science, one that related the spiritual (not yet specifically mental) to the physical realms (Murray 1988, 184). His work was much criticized at the time, but that he purported to be initiating a distinctly new science is clear.

Furthermore, recent research on the life and work of Wilhelm Wundt, often considered the father of modern experimental psychology, has revealed that the perception of his theory as positivist and mechanical in its description of internal behavioral causes is incorrect. It now seems likely that this picture has come largely through the work of the eminent historian of psychology, Edwin Boring (1929), who was a student of Edward Titchener, a student of Wundt. Titchener's version of Wundt's theory was thoroughly shaped by his own prejudices, and so he ignored prominent elements of Wundt's work that are more conspicuously mentalistic. For example, Wundt stressed the importance of the will in Volume III of *Ethics* and attacked associationism in the light of voluntarism in *Logic*. Another example of his explicit mentalism is his denial that the laws of psychic life are like the laws that apply to physical objects (Murray 1988, 206–209). Some may object that intimations of mentalism in early theorists of psychology, such as Freud or Wundt, merely illustrate their tentative and incomplete attempts to break free from unscientific thought forms. This view insists that from our later, more scientific vantage point, it is easy to sift out the vestiges of an older mentalism from a newly emerging (physicalist and positivist) framework for understanding behavior. This effort to purge psychology of all mentalism perhaps accounts for Titchener's filtering of Wundt's work.

But a modicum of thought reveals this view as presupposing that an antimentalist physicalism is the fundamental explanatory assumption in psychology. In fact, when early theorists like Wundt and Fechner and current writers like Rychlak use biological and medical language to discuss psychological phenomena, they do so metaphorically. This fact becomes evident from those passages in which they go beyond biological language in discussing the same phenomena. Simultaneously with physicalist explanations, they seek to develop a new vocabulary that does not rest on physical images, a vocabulary that is not yet fully formed; therefore, mental *illnesses* and mental *diseases* in time became mental *disorders*, with an emphasis on the disorder, or lack of it, between aspects of thought, feeling, and behavior. Instead of seeking a "cure," psychotherapy seeks a reordering or reintegration of personality. The term "mental disorder" thus avoids in some measure the connotation of biological causation and represents a truly psychological way of looking at this human problem.

THE EQUALITY OF PHYSICAL AND MENTAL PERSPECTIVES

For every mental event there is a correlative biological event. As far as we know, the nervous system changes in some way whenever a person acts or reports having had a feeling or a thought. But here is the difficult part: The majority of people in the Western world will take this truism as warrant for seeking the *origin* or *cause* of the mental event within the physical event instead of the other way around. Modern science has shifted toward interactive causation models within a cybernetic, complex, and dynamic array of causes for any particular event, but why is it not equally compelling in our scientific thinking to see a physical event as proceeding from a mental event? The answer we choose to give lies largely in our cultural prejudice favoring the physicalist explanation.

How mind interacts with body was a very real question for Leibnitz and, earlier, Rene Descartes. Descartes's goal was to solve the problem in order to—and this was important—preserve equal reality status for both mind and body. It was important to both philosophers that neither mind nor body be "lost." Biological and medical discoveries, and the ambient pre-Enlightenment thinking of Descartes's day, sought physical explanations for animal and human behavior. But Descartes knew that to accord unidirectional causation from brain to mind was tantamount to a materialist reductionism, to a denial of mind's existence. Leibnitz's psychophysical parallelism solution was an attempt to qualify that same fast-developing simplistic presupposition of the Enlightenment. Yet even today much so-called psychological thought proceeds on the unexamined presupposition of the sole reality of matter.

The care with which Gottfried Leibnitz, the eminent seventeenth-century German philosopher and scientist, stated his concern about and solution to the so-called mind/body problem sometimes perplexes students. His solution is sometimes called *psycho-physical parallelism*—the idea that body and soul are like two exactly synchronized clocks—and it accounted for what seemed to him to be the improbability of such different substances as mind and body affecting each another. Addressing this problem was not a philosopher's obsession with trivial pursuits but rather a very practical concern of the day (Titus 1953).

A telling example of this concern, and one that concretely influences generation after generation of college students, is the common practice of placing a chapter on the brain and other bodily systems affecting behavior toward the beginning of an introductory psychology textbook. Typically, this chapter is titled "The Biological Roots of Behavior," or something similar. Dozens of general psychology textbooks do this. But why should biology be accorded the status of behavior's roots? The term "roots" as well as the choice of placing the brain chapter toward the beginning of the books exhibits a somatic bias inconsistent with a genuine psychological perspective, erroneously supporting a derivative conception of the field.

This is not to deny the importance of brain and other somatic perspectives in psychological experience nor to ignore the extreme difficulty of fully discriminating mental from physical phenomena. As brain imaging techniques and their applications burgeon, specific kinds of behavior increasingly will be linked to brain changes. Moreover, links between brain states and behaviors have important implications for psychology; knowledge of them will be key to understanding many psychological phenomena.

But let it be said again: These findings are not part of psychology, or at most they are at psychology's margin. They are more properly behavioral biology. Psychology's unique mandate pertains to the influence and effects of *mind* on experience and behavior. Granted, to discover this influence and these effects, it is decidedly useful to consider a given behavior conceptualized also as biologically generated—that is, from a behavioral biology viewpoint. But the psychologist's distinctive work has only begun after a biology-behavior link has or has not been established; it certainly does not end there. And to that end, it might be a good temporary self-discipline if psychology would not even consider such findings as part of its own task-domain lest it delude itself about the extent to which an adequate explanation is provided by the discovery of biological correlates.

Let us consider a recent example. Biologist Simon LeVay (1991), in comparing hypothalamus cell clusters taken from deceased persons, discovered that those from homosexual men were significantly larger than those from heterosexual men. Whether the increased size of the clusters resulted from some aspect of homosexual behavior or whether homosexual behavior resulted from the increased size was not asked nor answered by his research. A separate but similar finding of larger *corpus callosums* in homosexual men is equally ambiguous as to direction of causation. These findings led naturally to the speculation that homosexuality is at least partly determined by biological, perhaps genetic, factors. This is indeed a reasonable speculation considering this and other important research findings.

Then it might be asked why such a finding should not be simply acknowledged and included in the domain of psychology, thus leaving the boundaries of psychology nicely open, permeable, and pragmatically ambiguous? The clear answer is that these biological formulations totally bypass *mind*, which is treated as either entirely superfluous or perhaps as a minor factor in understanding the fundamental dynamics of homosexual behavior. Disregarding mind in this research can be considered both reasonable and legitimate because the research has been done from a behavioral biology perspective. If it should happen that behavioral biology indeed provides all the answers society seeks regarding the origins of homosexuality, this considerable achievement should nonetheless be reckoned as falling outside the sphere of psychological research and knowledge. It is not psychology. However, if behavioral biology does not provide all the answers society seeks regarding the origins of homosexuality, it should be acknowledged that this research is behavioral biology, partly so that other psychological research findings premised on the existence and capacity of mind in human experience and behavior will be given their due status and credibility.

Another example is research on the neurophysiology of hunger and the treatment of eating disorders. The physiological concomitants of hunger were investigated during World War II using voluntary conscientious objectors as subjects. The food intake levels of these subjects were severely reduced to a semi-starvation level (Keys et al. 1950). The discovery from these experiments that subjects' general activity level and basal metabolic level allowed their body weight to stabilize at three-quarters of normal has been supported by much subsequent research on the physiology of eating, particularly on the role of the brain's hypothalamus (Duggan and Booth 1986). A set point of body weight seems to be established, and the hypothalamus regulates body weight so that it has a strong tendency to return to a relatively fixed body weight point.

This is clearly useful information for anyone, including psychologists, seeking to understand the nature of hunger or planning a treatment regimen for an eating disorder. But it is *cognate* information to psychology in the same sense that aspects of political science are important to students of history or that insights from sociology can critically inform religious studies. That is, a psychotherapeutic treatment of an eating disorder will principally have to do with the mind, with human choice and its functioning, not with neurophysiology. It is only our cultural fascination with "hard" sciences that inclines us to devote so much time and attention to a physical explanation in lieu of an explanation in which we have much less trust—one that is genuinely psychological. When in their writing and research psychologists fail to make these discriminations, they signal to the broader society the superiority of a physicalist explanation and the inferior and perhaps temporary status of a psychological one. Psychology, some think, is a method to use until the doctor arrives.

The discipline of psychology needs to be more courageous in its commitment to mentalist theoretical formulations. So long as it pretends that physicalist formulations are an integral part of its own self-definition, it will risk, in both the research and delivery-of-services arenas, an almost inevitably unfavorable comparison with neuroscience and neuropsychiatry. This would be a lose-lose choice for psychologists. More seriously for the entire society, the unique and much-needed contribution that psychology is able to make would be obscured by its second-class expertise in biomedical knowledge and research.

The relatively small subset of psychologists who have made neurobiology their life's work should not be ignored. Clearly, there is a group of psychologists whose training and knowledge is second to none in brain anatomy, physiology, and imaging interpretation. But their expertise is in no danger of being lost to research if a shift in psychology's self-definition were to locate them just outside the perimeter of psychology and more appropriately in behavioral biology, either neuropsychiatry or brain science research. Psychologists will always be interested in their research.

LENINIST PSYCHOLOGY: A MATERIALIST VERSION

Materialism has never been an official public philosophy in European or American countries, however large a part it may actually play in the values and thinking of those countries' citizens. But it is instructive to consider how psychology developed under a political regime that self-consciously professed materialism (dialectic materialism) as a matter of official ideology: the Soviet Union after 1917. Although psychology systems that took the mind seriously continued to develop and even flourish in the West, those same ideas, and especially psychoanalysis, were banned from official instruction in the USSR, presumably because they did not fit with a pure materialist view of personality. What was offered instead were entirely physicalist approaches to behavior, with the work of Ivan Pavlov as the best known representative of these approaches.

Because of the Soviet Union's explicit profession of a materialist worldview, it is essential to address the strong commitment to a mechanist psychology that prevailed during the Communist regime (Boring 1950).

This was in great contrast with the intellectual milieu of Russia in the nineteenth century. The work of physiologist Ivan M. Sechenov (1829–1905) illustrates mechanism well. Prior to the revolution, Sechenov researched the suppression of reflexes in frogs (Murray 1988, 306). He discovered that if a frog's brain was sectioned at the level of the optic thalami, stimulating the sectioned areas would suppress the scratch reflex.

Sechenov believed that this demonstration of reflex inhibition had ramifications for understanding voluntary human behavior and thought. He presented these ideas in an 1863 monograph entitled *Reflexes of the Brain*. His line of thought offended Russian censors, who rightly detected its mechanistic and antivolunteerist nature. They also reasoned that according to this view, people eventually would be excused from moral responsibility for their actions (Murray 1988, 307). The prerevolutionary Russian perspective on personhood still included personal agency and responsibility, and it was not yet ready to ignore the mind in favor of the nervous system as the locus of individual control.

In 1917, Marxism/Leninism officially authorized philosophical materialism as a fundamental axiom of Communist economics. As such, Sechenov's reductionist constructions for human behavior became welcome, as did the later work of Ivan Pavlov (1849–1936) and Vladimir Bekhterev (1857–1927). It is interesting to note the boldness with which Pavlov expressed his lack of patience for interpretations, like those of the Gestaltists, that imply mental activities of a truly psychological sort:

> In the last decade or so of Pavlov's life, regular meetings were held in his laboratory every Wednesday morning and records were kept of the conversations. . . . [I]n these meetings he was very critical of Gestalt theory. For Pavlov, Kohler's apes were not "thinking" in those quiescent moments in their problem-solving activities; they were merely resting. (Murray 1988, 313)

Bekhterev was more systematic than Pavlov in the effort to apply mechanistic reflex theory to higher psychological phenomena such as imitation, speech, and voluntary activity. It is clear that an official disbelief in the existence of mind (or spirit) under the Soviets resulted in a simplified version of the psychology that was simultaneously developing in the United States within the behaviorist movement. Halting attempts to develop a science of true psychology were severely restricted by the materialist mechanism espoused by biology. Any hint of teleological explanation for biological events, including animal and human behavior, was distinctly unwelcome (Murray 1988).

COMPARABLE DEVELOPMENTS IN THE WEST

In the United States and England at the beginning of the century, psychology attempted to carve out a domain of its own. Its ambivalence about becoming autonomous from medicine and psychiatry was expressed in the behavior therapy movement of the 1950s. Searching for an alternative to the dominant medical model—including psychoanalysis, which had been adopted by psychiatry, thus identifying it professionally with medicine—behavior therapy held promise of being a respectable alternative to both because of its materialistic mechanism (Glass and Arnkoff 1992).

Although there were some physicians in the forefront of behavior therapy research, preeminent among whom was Joseph Wolpe, most of those who originated and developed behavior therapy methods were psychologists. Commanding widespread popular interest, behavior therapy was psychology's first public success. For a time, it rivaled Rogers's client-centered approach as an alternative to the medical model and psychoanalysis. Although psychology thereby found a measure of popular and medical acceptance in the only mechanistic psychotherapy model available, behavior therapy was not far removed from the physiology in which it had its roots. Its credibility still lay in the proposed reflexology applications of Sechenov, Pavlov, Behkterev, and the radical antimentalism of B.F. Skinner. In behavior therapy, the discipline of psychology made progress toward more complete autonomy from medicine and psychiatry; unfortunately, it did so within a continuing biomedical, physicalist mode.

OTHER OBSTACLES TO DEMEDICALIZING PSYCHOLOGY

A clearer definition of psychology and psychotherapy focusing primarily on *mind* rather than body has become increasingly difficult to attain over the past three decades. The burgeoning of brain science resulting from such discoveries as sophisticated imaging techniques and the promise of DNA decoding for certain brain anomalies commands center stage for both psychologists and other behavioral scientists. To some, rapid advances in psychopharmacology suggest that the future of influencing human behavior lies in the use of chemical agents. In fact, some psychologists are pressing federal and state legislators to allow them prescription privileges. Although the current esteem accorded cognitive approaches to therapy *combined* with behavorist ones is encouraging (Lazarus 1991), totally mentalistic systems of psychology such as psychoanalysis are in disfavor as we approach the twenty-first century.

Another obstacle to developing a psychology that studies mind is a practical one that concerns authority structures within the mental health professions. Despite considerable progress in establishing the autonomy of clinical psychology from psychiatry in the delivery of a wide range of services, government-regulated restructuring of Medicare and Medicaid payments through large health maintenance organizations has further formalized significant fee discrepancies among mental health care professions. Apart from the question of economic fairness, these discrepancies tend to legitimatize the superiority of psychiatry and medicine among the psychotherapy professions.

Here again the issue of mind as conceptually separate from body is crucial. If it were generally accepted that psychology is the profession *specifically* dedicated to researching the mind (not the brain) and to treating its dysfunctions, then it is arguable that the psychologist should be accorded first place on the therapy team. As a result, treatment modes that are important but do *not* specifically focus on mind—medicine, social work, spiritual counseling—might reasonably be regarded as important adjunctive services to psychotherapy. For all that, this is not an argument for making the psychologist the most prestigious or highest paid member of the team. An egalitarian rewarding system would work best for all concerned: professionals *and* consumers. It *is*, however, an argument for no longer tacitly assuming that the psychiatrist is best qualified to lead the team and therefore should be paid more than others.

By contrast, the commonly held reductionist view that mental processes can and will someday be fully understood or treatable in physical terms (brain functions, hormonal balances, neurotransmitter effects, etc.) makes mental theories potentially superfluous for the future. This trend naturally would place psychiatrists/neurologists in the commanding position when the scientific kingdom has fully come.[5] The regard in which a society holds a given professional—teacher, shaman, doctor, lawyer, priest—is not only an indicator of its value hierarchy but also of its belief structure. When two professions work closely in tandem on the same human problems, but one profession is clearly esteemed more highly than the other, modal beliefs undergirding the professions are reflected. In the case of psychotherapy, a tacit physicalism currently reigns with respect to understanding and treating psychological disorders.

RESEARCH ON THE SELF AND SELF-ESTEEM

Nonetheless, it is clear that mentalism/human choice *has* made some advances in recent decades simultaneously with impressive advances in brain science. An important aspect of these advances, in addition to the study of higher cognitive processes, has been research on the self, especially therapeutic benefits associated with increasing the esteem accorded to the self. Carefully note that the self is clearly *not* a physical entity and therefore not amenable to medical intervention; however, its investigation has yielded important insight into psychotherapy. This provisional reifying of a psychological construct, not unlike what Freud did with the id, ego, and superego, has been accepted by many psychologists and others in the broader society who are willing to give it a "real" status. This is a hopeful sign.

Beginning in the 1970s, research focusing on the self structure has become one of psychology's most popular topics. During 1993, *Psychological Abstracts* referenced 5396 articles and books about the self (Myers 1995, 482). However, human *agency* (choice-making capacity) is at the core of both mind and self, rendering the concepts functionally equivalent for many purposes. Although the term mind (or mental) passed into disfavor with psychologists in the early part of the twentieth century, it takes little more than sleight of hand to replace the construct *mind* with *self*. This is not to say that the substitution of terms has been deliberately deceptive. Rather it is a convenient way to avoid the unpopular mentalist concept and to dodge the centrally perceived problem: the implied presence of an homunculus (active chooser) within the individual who is proactive rather than reactive. Research on the *self* for some reason seems exempt from the age-old agency problem.

Still wary of mentalism, psychologists have concocted this and other clever ways of preserving human agency without seeming to preserve it. Awkward as these efforts are, we should applaud and encourage them. Most of them imply that agency consists in a subjective (but erroneous) belief in self-control on the subject's part. For example, Albert Bandura (1986) refers to "reciprocal determinism." By this he means that personal/cognitive factors interact with both environmental and behavioral factors to shape psychological experience. The implication is that personal/cognitive factors can be identified and studied, just as they have been in the past; however, this process will not necessarily yield predictive power because the picture is vastly complicated by environmental and behavioral factors. The three factors, in countless combinations, can result in interaction effects that are difficult to predict. Thus the complexity of central personhood (agency), the meta-function that governs the complex picture managing to steer the organism to a desired outcome, is hinted at without quite being stated. It is a step toward acknowledging mind.

Other examples are the Learned Helplessness concept of Seligman (1975, 1991) and the Locus of Control research (e.g., Benassi et al. 1988; Rotter 1966). Seligman shows that if individuals develop feelings and beliefs of powerlessness concerning the self, they will act powerlessly. The feelings and beliefs themselves are the predictive factors. Seligman stops short of asserting or denying that the self or the mind actually exists.

Similarly, Rotter's Internal Locus of Control-oriented subjects, believing the determinants of their fate are within themselves, consistently achieve more in school, show less depression, and live life more effectively than do "externals." Again, the question is begged as to whether control *actually* lies within the individual; the predictive factors are the subject's beliefs about whether they do or not. In this system, too, mind is implied, but asserting it is avoided and is not considered essential to the system.

Significantly, asserting self/mind is not *in*compatible with these systems. Joseph Rychlak (1988) has spelled out this approach with philosophical detail and logical consistency in what he calls "Logical Learning Theory." In elaborating his idea of agency, he says,

The human image which validly emerges in research on [Logical Learning Theory] is that of a telosponsive organism, capable of both arbitrariness and rigid determinism in its behavior, furthering meanings for the sake of which it behaves in both preferred and nonpreferred directions. Life experience is ordered by an agent known as the *person* or *self* who actively conceptualizes from the protopoint. [emphasis added] (482).

In these and other ways the cognitive revolution has begun to help restore the mind to its rightful place as the focus of psychological investigation.

POSTMODERNISM AS A FRESH OPPORTUNITY FOR PSYCHOLOGY

Many studies of intellectual history place the modern period immediately following, and in stark contrast to, the medieval period. Whereas medieval thought was dominated by authority as the source of truth, the modern period was empirical, positivist, and materialist, seeking truth through the verification processes that we call science (Bernstein 1983). Many agree that we have now moved into a postmodern period in which the premises of the positivist scientific tradition have been rejected and replaced with a new approach to science and knowledge.

Because postmodernism is in its early stages, it is presently unclear exactly what will replace the modernist approach to truth seeking. There are several possibilities. For our purposes, the important factor is that the practice of a particular science or social science will be different in the twenty-first century. Whether the change is termed a deconstructed psychology, a paradigmatic shift, or a dialogical interaction with other interpretive traditions, it is clear that new directions will soon be available for psychology, including reintroducing mind and self into the fabric of psychological theory, research, and practice.[6]

Particularly relevant here is the materialism closely associated with the positivist methodology that characterized modernism. For decades, a powerful influence and controlling assumption on psychological theorizing has been that *hypothetical constructs* are superior to *intervening variables*—a distinction first clarified by MacCorquodale and Meehl (1948). These authors defined a hypothetical construct as a psychological idea for which a corresponding bodily process or structure, probably in the brain, might be discoverable.

Thus when researching appetitive behavior, a theorist might propose a hunger center having certain characteristics. If it was proposed because it seemed likely that such a center in the brain, along with its processes, could be identified, the idea was considered a hypothetical construct. As such it was regarded as more significant and bearing more followup investigation than an intervening variable. This proved to be the case, for example, with the discovery of the lateral and ventromedial hypothalamus.

An intervening variable, on the other hand, had no concomitant physical entity to which it was isomorphic. It was usually an abstraction representing several experimental operations. If a theorist proposed a Need for Belonging, as did Maslow, for which it seemed unlikely that a physical structure would be discovered, the idea constituted an intervening variable and was defined by one or more research operations. As such, it was regarded as vaguer, somewhat metaphysical, more ephemeral, and more difficult to investigate using the methods of science.

In positivist terms, Need for Belonging is a shorthand reference to a set of operations. An intervening variable thus seems more difficult to investigate because of the specific operational definition needed before any research can be done. Because of this situation, Maslow (1979) often complained of the second-class citizenship accorded his concepts. Hypothetical constructs are less exacting in their need for operationalization because a *physical* structure or process *is* under investigation and its biological basis eventually *is* discoverable. Again, the biological explanation is given automatic preference.

This bias stems from the greater degree of reality ascribed by our culture to the physical realm of tangible entities—the realm from which observation of pure fact is supposedly derived. The modern scientific set of assumptions about reality included the superiority of matter along with skepticism about anything that was *not* matter. This presupposition is so deeply ingrained in the modern mind that it remains difficult to raise the issue for serious examination. Indeed, the reader may register surprise when asked to question this assumption.

To break this concept down further, fact was considered the foundation of science; only matter could be truly factual. Other knowledge was built on the shifting sands of faith, feeling, or speculation. To believe in spiritual or mental reality required a leap of faith that the scientifically minded did not feel a need to make. The psychological community marginalized those who took a different position. The collapse of foundationalism has promised to change this picture (Wolterstorff 1976). The indubitables of modernism, the cornerstone of unquestionable truths on which all of science is built, do not exist. Descartes's program of building such a base for all knowledge has not succeeded. This means that what defines a reliable fact is less clear in postmodern thought. Such ambiguity also calls into question the modernist connection between matter and fact. For example, because a fact in chemistry and a fact in economics may now be seen as sharing a common uncertainty or a lower level of certainty, it is not at all clear to a postmodernist that the fact in chemistry is of a different and superior order than the fact in economics.

From the viewpoint of those of us who see mind, agency, or personhood as central to our enterprise, this spells a happy liberation for psychology. The discipline is released from its self-imposed obligation to ape the physical sciences, a need that has bedeviled psychology from its origins. Although it may usefully employ the new findings from brain science, pharmacology research, and genetic discoveries, it need not derive its raison d'etre from them. It is autonomous of them. If psychologists will recognize their distinctive identity and so accept their destiny, future biochemists may be borrowing expertise from psychology in attempting to interpret their findings just as the reverse happens today. A healthy dialogue already exists between cognitive psychologists and biologists working on specific disorders such as depression (Elkin et al. 1989).

This move will require a greater humility from those who have most strongly identified with modern versus postmodern science. That includes those working within the ranks of psychology who have strongly advocated logical positivist methods of natural science as well as the natural scientists working alongside psychology, especially physicians and psychiatrists. The hubris represented by expectations of superior status and remuneration should be recognized as inappropriate to a postmodern understanding of human knowledge, both biological and psychological.

Psychology's Distinctive Mandate

It is instructive that more than 70 percent of research on schizophrenia reported at the 1993 International Congress on Schizophrenia was primarily biological (Iacono and Grove 1993). In this "decade of the brain," many perceive the most promising clues to the nature of all mental disorders to be medical/biological. Because none of us can predict how much fruit they will bear, all of these biological leads should be followed with diligence.

But psychologists have a different mandate, one that takes seriously the complex functioning and potential for disorder of the self, the personal mind, rather than the brain. Whether the self is well-functioning or disordered, psychologists' working assumption is that mind will be manifest in body just as truly as body will be manifest in mind. If body or behavior can be investigated through biological methods independently of mind, which few would dispute, psychologists hold that mind can and should be investigated in a similarly independent way. Again, I do not minimize how strange this statement sounds to our contemporary ears.

Medicine is historically responsible, through psychoanalysis, for pioneering the important idea that a domain of the mind exists apart from the domain of the spirit. At the turn of the twentieth century, this was a new and disturbing idea to many. Medicine ought to be justly proud of this major achievement. Sigmund Freud was largely responsible for this significant breakthrough in our cultural understanding.

But that idea needed to be carefully elaborated and extended. Medicine was and is ill equipped for the task. Psychiatry was not armed with the philosophic expertise it needed to sustain its argument and to move the idea forward. By contrast, psychology grew from both biology and philosophy. Many of the early psychologists were well trained in both disciplines; therefore, the mandate was passed to psychology. This mandate was to value and explore mind, rather than spirit or body.

Returning to a developmental metaphor, like growing children ambivalent about separation from their parents, psychology needs to take the next step in leaving the nest. Medicine's attraction continues to be its established prestige, its clear accomplishment, and its financial security. It is tempting for psychology to wish to function under medicine's protection, defining itself as a paramedical discipline. Many psychologists have decided to do just that, carving out a pleasant, comfortable niche for themselves. Perhaps this dependency was an important phase in the development of psychology as a service profession. Certainly a cooperative relationship with medicine will always be important. But psychology needs to remember its special identity, which holds that people have minds that can be investigated with empirical methods appropriately modified to their subject matter.

I close this chapter by focusing on a quote from neuroscientist Roger Sperry (1985): "Everything in science to date seems to indicate that conscious awareness is a property of the living functioning brain and inseparable from it." As we look at his statement, consider that Sperry is a prominent, thoughtful, and value-sensitive brain researcher. However, Sperry's words illustrate how difficult even he finds it to escape the tyranny of physicalism in theories of human behavior.

In the quotation, Sperry goes beyond an appropriate interpretation of brain research data in two ways. First, an abundance of religious and quasi-religious human traditions—ancient and modern, primitive and sophisticated—have persisted in affirming conscious awareness in beings who are not physical, for example, in God. Regardless of how thoroughly Sperry and others may have investigated neural functions, they have little cause for ruling these traditions wrong on the basis of their research. Such a ruling is outside their methodology and is far too sweeping a generalization to affirm with any degree of certainty. It is instructive that at the end of the twentieth century, Sperry is still willing to make such a statement. It is even more instructive that others are willing to quote him as an authority on this question.

Second, and more important for our purposes, Sperry's discovery of the "inseparable" connection between psychological experience and "the living functioning brain" impels him to conclude that "conscious awareness is a property of" the brain. Conversely, could the brain's functioning be a property of conscious awareness (mind)? Despite how unfamiliar and strange the concept seems to us, it could be true. This strangeness has nothing to do with any supposed discoveries during this century that the cosmos and the people living in it are mindless. The fact is that such a discovery cannot be made. Instead, the *assumption* that the cosmos and the person are mindless has become pervasive in popular thought both inside and outside intellectual circles. It is now the normal way to look at life.

My argument is not for the hegemony of mind over body in our general thinking. It is only a plea that mind be researched as autonomous and important equitably with body. And this is psychology's special and peculiar mandate.

NOTES

1. Medicine's social status was clearly headed on its upward trajectory by the end of the nineteenth century. If psychology had begun its development in the eighteenth century when medicine was just developing, it would probably have felt less of a need to distinguish itself from medicine and more of a need to distinguish itself from religion. As it happened, widespread religious skepticism in early twentieth-century academia provided a ready-made way for psychology to distance itself more easily from religion.

2. More specifically, Michael Polanyi (1958) has pointed out in his emergence theory that there are different levels of being and knowing (though one may emerge from another), and what is real at one level cannot be known by investigating what is real at other levels, either above or below it. This is another way to account for what I mean by the ontological equivalence of mind, spirit, and matter.

3. It is significant that this exclusion has been recently tested in the United States judicial system with the finding that such nonmedical trainees should be granted access (DeAngelis 1989). Both psychoanalytic and nonpsychoanalytic psychologists recognize this ruling as an important token of psychology's autonomy from medicine.

Access to psychoanalytic training by any broadly educated person is just and reasonable because there is no direct connection between medical treatment and the psychoanalytic constructs of personality or development proposed by Freud.

4. Freud did not have the benefit of modern emergence theory by which to conceptualize how the physical might relate to the psychological in human knowledge. While my perspective on Freud seems somewhat revisionist, I believe there is evidence that Freud would have been willing to separate his concepts of the mind from the physical stratum if there had not been interpersonal rivalry issues complicating his view. This is, of course, speculation.

5. Again, I am referring to "eliminatist" reductionism to which many people, both professional and lay, are inclined.

6. One of the first thorough attempts to take advantage of the open door of postmodern opportunity was by George Mandler in his work *Mind and Body* (1984), in which he strives to put all the strands of past psychological traditions together with notions of consciousness and personhood.

4

Psychology in Contrast with Social Work

*T*he premise of a psychology that takes mind seriously also has implications for the discipline's relationship to social work. As an application of sociology to specific human problems, social work operates from a perspective that assumes the central importance of social influences in the etiology and solution of these problems.[1] In actual practice, social work is like psychology in its inclusion of other perspectives—the psychological and the physical. But at its core, membership of the individual in groups is social work's peculiar interest and mandate.

In place of personal agency, where individual mind perceives, assesses, and makes behavioral choices, social work sees the individual as part of a social system that can be understood as an organismic whole. This is a legitimate and valuable perspective that has enriched our picture of human behavior. Perhaps *the* primary example of this perspective is the ingenious social/economic/political formulation of Karl Marx (although Marx was clearly not a social worker as we normally use that term).

Because of the growing prevalence of philosophic materialism in the Western world at the beginning of the twentieth century, Marx's *dialectical materialism* was an important bridge for the modern mind in conceptualizing how material reality could be socially and personally influential. In this sense, it supplemented the idealist and physicalist account of psychological events, strengthening the physicalist account by adding another way to see matter as "all that matters."

According to the Marxian economic/political account, the greatest influence on the lives of citizens has to do with the availability of social power in the form of capital (Marx and Engels 1848/1967). Marxian theory asserts that capitalism encourages hoarding of power by a relative few, leaving the rest of the population deprived. For the Marxist, the primary task of good government is to prevent this from happening, ensuring that capital is distributed fairly to all.

I could cite many other social theories in which the individual simply plays a functional role in a larger system, including the sociological formulations of Max Weber (1930) and the earlier free market economic formulations of Adam Smith (1776). Each of these theories has its own set of presuppositions about the nature of the human individual that allows it to predict average behaviors (not particular ones) on which it makes actuarial projections about the societal, economic, political, or social direction of the group. These perspectives typically spell out some of the ways in which the participating individual is influenced to comply with group needs and expectations and thus predict individual behavior.

For our purposes, this chapter will focus on the contrast between this nomothetic approach that predicts individual behavior according to group norms, and what in psychology is the more distinctively idiographic mode of research that studies the individual's behavioral patterns to make predictions just about this unique person. This distinction between nomothetic and idiographic approaches was first introduced by Gordon Allport (1961) in his attempt to highlight the study of personality as an entity that is not simply viewed as part of a larger social whole. His own way of doing this was through trait theory, but other styles of pursuing idiographic research, including developmental and clinical studies, center on the complexity and richness of personal mental experience. Idiographic research supplements nomothetic research, both psychological and sociological.

SOCIAL EXPLANATION FOR BEHAVIOR AND EXPERIENCE

At the risk of some oversimplification, I propose the following statement: The religionist seeks the causes of behavior and experience in *spirit*; the physicalist seeks them in *body*; the social theorist seeks them in *group membership*. All three of these perspectives have obvious merit, but none is a psychological account/explanation and none should be mistaken for one. Psychology would benefit from a more laser-like focus on the person as agent.

College-level general psychology textbooks present a fair number of studies that confusingly assume a sociological or social work perspective, an interdisciplinary blurring not limited to psychology. Comparable sections of introductory social work textbooks feature lengthy accounts of psychological theories, typically presented without signaling to the reader the difference in disciplinary perspectives presented.

This untroubled ignoring of boundaries is different from legitimate inclusion within psychology of authentic social psychology studies that examine the perceptions and responses of the person relative to a given social milieu. Social psychology is not sociology applied to the individual; it is the study of the *individual* as she or he perceives, thinks about, and interacts with others in groups.

Sociology and social work presuppose a certain reality inherent in the group per se, the basic nature of human society, and the processes that result in both continuity and change. As disciplines, they might be said to reify the *group* in the same way I propose psychology ought to reify the *mind*. This premise provides sociology with its distinctive, dynamic perspective that has given us valuable insights about our common social life. For sociology, it is the group, small or large, that assumes an organismic life, and it is the individual who becomes a functional component of that life. It would be most unfortunate if sociology were to forego, neglect, or fail to develop its unique premise concerning human life and experience. It needs the discipline to assume its distinctive viewpoint and see where that viewpoint takes it.

Social *psychology* does not fully assume this perspective but focuses instead on the person, albeit the person profoundly influenced by memberships and interactions. It sees the person as having incorporated into his/her personality specific aspects of group membership.

Again the question arises: Why take care to preserve disciplinary boundaries? The answer relates not so much to particular research findings as it does to clarity of thought about the implications of those findings.

Maintaining disciplinary boundaries helps us to keep in mind our peculiar presuppositions. In the case of sociology, we presuppose that the group as such has a certain reality of its own. Insofar as we can affirm this premise, sociological research findings will have greater force for us, and more telling implications. But not everyone will affirm the premise with equal conviction. Those who have more difficulty affirming it will find sociological research data and their derived social work applications less compelling than those who can affirm it with ease. The same is true of psychology: Those who can affirm the existence of mind with a fairly broad latitude in defining what that means will find studies having a genuinely psychological perspective more persuasive and consequential than those who cannot affirm it. Disciplinary boundaries help us to simultaneously affirm and reexamine our basic presuppositions. Disciplinary diffusion encourages us to ignore and leave unexamined such presuppositions.

But our concern in this book is more with psychologists who desert their identity and function as social workers. Without questioning the enormous value of the sociological and/or social work perspective, psychology looks at behavior "as though" it were arising from within individuals, or at least from within individuals in the process of construing their social reality. Family systems theory presupposes a primary influence of the group as enforced through family role membership. When modified to recognize the complex threads of family influence on the individual's thinking and feelings—this could be a psychological perspective—family systems theory can be most helpful. But the psychologist cannot practice family systems in its pure form without forsaking his or her true professional identity.

THE PRACTICE OF GROUP THERAPY

As psychology has developed its popular identity in the mid- and late twentieth century, one of its most identifiable service features has been offering therapy and personal growth groups. But to what extent is this development concordant with psychology's essential assertion of mind and personal agency?

The popularity of groups of all kinds—therapy, growth, and self-help—suggests the pervasiveness of basic human needs for belonging, mutual support, mutual criticism, and social comparison (Rosenbaum, Lakin, and Roback 1992). Groups are appropriate venues for exploring and meeting these needs. The social skills required to meet these needs in an ongoing way can best be acquired in a group context that reinforces such learning through simultaneously meeting those personal needs.

There is, however, a concept of therapy group process that is inimical to psychology's identity. The most extreme example are groups formed specifically to influence some aspect of a society's practice or attitude. Ethnotherapy groups, for example, strive to raise the consciousness of group members and outsiders influenced by members about the underrated value of a given ethnic tradition. Gender therapy groups exist to encourage sharing of experiences and exploration of discontent with a current gender role and have the goal of helping members decide on particular social actions they must take to remedy the social failing.

Such groups very likely fulfill a valuable social function and are much needed. But is the conduct of such groups appropriate to *psychology's* distinctive avowal of personal agency or mind? In these groups, personal psychological difficulties are assumed to stem from group differences. A single social issue, thought of as residing in the society and not in the individual, is presupposed as the source of a range of negative consequences. Personal insights about personal concerns are not the focus. In discussing this issue, Rosenbaum et al. (1992) make the point that this "global characterization of individual psychological problems (results in) the delegitimization of individual differences" (717). Thus, for example, a group dedicated to problems of gender, ethnicity, codependency, alcoholism, spousal abuse, or anger control has a tendency to submerge idiosyncratic features of individual members as the group investigates elements of the social problem.

This kind of group theory is a natural application of social work ideology, but it does not fit psychology. The assumption that a recognizable syndrome of personal disorders is directly attributable to group membership is a cogent hypothesis but one that is more appropriate to social work/sociology than to psychology. For psychology, the change sought is within the person. When psychology uses group work, the purpose is to explore and harness the influence of the group, as perceived by the person, to bring about personal change.

Investigating social influence is fully consistent with a psychology emphasizing personal agency. Social psychology may investigate a wide range of factors that all come to focus on the "clearinghouse" of the mind, and each of the social factors is not simplistically construed as having an independent impact on a person's behavior and experience. Instead, each factor is viewed as modifying the complex operations of the mind in an interactive mix with a host of other influences. Although it is possible statistically to parcel out the effect of a single input variable on a particular outcome variable, a genuinely psychological perspective will bear in mind the difficult-to-predict interactive effects of any given variable when combined within a complex and ever-attentive mind. This means, for example, that the psychological effects of gender, ethnicity, or social class are not easily identified in a particular person. Idiographic methods are called for.

It is appropriate for social psychology empirically to investigate attitudes, conformity, obedience, group influence, aggression, altruism, attraction, and other phenomena of social influence. Psychology will account for behavior (e.g., decisions, reported experience, feelings) as the product of the individual mind construing group life; social work or sociology, working under quite a different set of assumptions, accounts for behavior as an expression of group life. The difference between these perspectives is not always apparent in the conduct and reporting of an empirical study, but the subtle differences are amplified when the study's implications are explored and interpreted for practical purposes of intervention.

Ignoring personal agency in order to simplify the experimental picture has often proven irresistible to research psychologists. Examples include explaining individual behavior on the basis of socioeconomic level, gender, ethnicity, alcoholism, or subcultural attitude. To discover a direct correlational or causal link between an input and output variable seems eminently scientific. Happily, in recent decades the statistical concepts of multivariate causation and interaction (curvilinear) effects have begun to help researchers describe the complexity of mind in a way more consistent with psychology's historical commitment. The cognitive revolution sprang indirectly from this reawakened awareness of the core identity of psychology.

EVOLUTIONARY PSYCHOLOGY AND MIND

In a sense, the twentieth century has been a long experiment in testing two competing corollary versions of evolutionary theory. One version asserts that millennia of human experience have resulted in human societies that *as groups* embody the survival behaviors to which individual groups members accede. In this corollary, the group, because it contains the norm as none of its individual members does or could, is more "real" than the individual. This perspective is basic, for example, to Marxian and other distinctly sociological formulations.

The other theory asserts that the evolutionary process and experience has resulted in *individual* humans who, whether in groups or alone, possess minds capable of assessing meaning and then personally acting on that meaning. In this version of evolutionary outcome, the person is viewed as logically prior to—more "real" than—the group. Francis Galton (Charles Darwin's cousin) is correctly considered an early prototypic figure for psychological investigators as he focused on individual differences in mental abilities. In this theory, the fruit of evolutionary change is located within each person in the form of the capacity for freedom of choice. This perspective on individual difference powerfully shaped early psychological formulations.

So, for example, the study of helping behavior may be considered from an evolutionary psychology viewpoint (Rushton 1989). In such an analysis, the question becomes how a particular mental tendency contributes to the survival primarily of the individual and secondarily of the group. Looking at helping behavior in this way casts some light on why individual differences exist and even on how they may be modified. This psychological viewpoint is sharply in contrast to one that attributes the distinctive variables in helping behavior mostly to the group.

There is no dispute about the existence of group norms for behavior, nor that such norms influence individual behavior. The psychological perspective, however, does not grant that the group constitutes an organismic reality in and of itself and that it exercises a predictable influence on individual members. That is a social work perspective. From a genuinely psychological viewpoint, group norms are nothing more or less than tacit or explicit agreements among group members as to expectations and standards enforceable by various means within the group. Group norms do not have a reality in themselves.

This discussion leads naturally to the query, why must there be an either/or approach to the sociological versus psychological perspectives? Why not combine the two or hold an interactive dialogue? This kind of eclectic and seemingly synergistic approach is widespread, appealing, and well in accord with the currently highly valued pluralism. Why challenge it?

My answer is partly a matter of intellectual style or preference that values staying within a disciplinary framework. Beyond that, I believe that postulating the psychological assumption leads to different conclusions from those arrived at by postulating the social work assumption. Our current understanding of science informs us that it is impossible to say which assumption is more in accord with reality. What *is* possible and preferable is to keep the two lines of reasoning, psychology and social work (both research and practice), somewhat separate in order to adequately determine to what conclusions each comes when pursued thoroughly and consistently.

Animal forms evolve within groups, but the individual animal is typically considered the critical unit of the evolutionary process. This means that to understand a particular psychological event it is essential to postulate just how that event ensures or undermines an individual animal's survival long enough to pass on genes to progeny. Thus Darwin and Galton explored how the adaptation of the individual to a given environment, along with particulars of thinking, feeling, and behaving, led to a greater likelihood of parent and offspring survival.

This individual adaptive capacity has become axiomatic in modern psychological theory with the emphasis on features of the mind that assist adaptation. Jean Piaget (1972) and Sigmund Freud (1927) both took it as one of their starting points. Freud assumed that these adaptive functions were largely unconscious and studied them as such. Piaget attempted to specify how adaptive intelligence grows normally through childhood to its full capacity. Exploring the mental functions underlying adaptation to the demands of social or physical environments defined psychology in its early history and still provides its most powerful unifying theme.

Sociological knowledge about dynamics within and among social groups—racial, ethnic, language, ideological, cultural—has enhanced psychology's investigation of the mind as the social counterpart to the mind's operations. As sociology has provided more information about group functioning, social psychologists have been able to describe coping responses in distinctively psychological terms, resulting in studies of attribution, attitude, suggestibility, conformity, obedience, the presence of others, aggression, altruism, and attraction. How the mind processes social events remains the rightful focus in all these investigations.

CONTIGUOUS DISCIPLINES AND PSYCHOLOGY'S IDENTITY STRUGGLE

Several writers have addressed the need for thoughtful dialogue about the private and public identity of psychology. Altman (1987) addresses psychology's need to clarify its identity by describing centripetal and centrifugal trends in the discipline. He feels the period from 1900 through 1960 represents a centripetal era of psychology that focused primarily on its unifying themes and so established an integrated identity, both for itself and for outsiders. After 1960, he notes, many questions were raised about the nature of psychology, questions that paralleled the radical self-examination Western societies experienced during the 1960s and 1970s. Altman believes this post-1960s period is marked by disorganization and increased individualism in the way psychology is construed and taught, especially at the graduate level. Strife and excessive pluralism have resulted within the discipline.

A major training conference was convened in Salt Lake City, Utah, in 1987, to consider the direction of professional education in psychology; it also addressed this issue of psychology's identity, as had earlier conferences in Boulder and Vail, Colorado (Cohen 1992). The Salt Lake City conference naturally and unavoidably moved beyond a mere consideration of the applied branches of psychology to give serious attention to the discipline per se. One of the conference's four themes was the relative absence of and need for *unity* in psychology. Cognate to this need is the question of whether a central corpus of psychological knowledge exists, and on what grounds it may be thought of as internally integrated. The conference chose a hands-off policy with regard to specifying the curricula of academic psychology departments, but it did recommend a detailed core curriculum for students preparing for a delivery-of-services career that requires licensing or certification.

Not often considered in discussions like the Utah conference is the influence on psychology of disciplines such as social work that are contiguous to it on a day-to-day working basis. This daily interaction is a potentially powerful shaper of psychology's identity. One reason for the diminishing sense of unity in psychology is the common and erroneous assumption that psychotherapy is the same process whether practiced by a psychiatrist, a cleric, a psychologist, or a social worker. Because each of these disciplines begins with distinctive presuppositions that differ substantially, and because these presuppositions inevitably shape any resulting implementation, the generic use of the term "psychotherapy" for all four disciplines is inappropriate.[2] In the interest of congenial cooperation and because there are not enough specific labels for workers in each mental health specialty, the myth has been widely promulgated that all such workers engage in basically the identical process when addressing personal problems, although each does so with a distinctive twist. This assumption is evident in the frequent unqualified use of the term "psychotherapist." However, professionals are aware of differences in approaches resulting in an ongoing power struggle among the four types of workers. In discussing the mental health team, Riess (1992) quotes an observation by Schwartz:

> As to the dynamics of the three professions, the occupational hazard of being a psychotherapist is the God complex. The psychiatrist knows he is God; the psychologist wants to be God. The psychiatrist and the psychologist are in titanic conflict as to who will be God on the mental health Olympus. Only the social worker abstains from overt engagement in the battle before the totem feast. She does not enter into the struggle as to who will be God-the-Father. She is content to be the Mother of God. (768)

Construing as a simple power struggle the deep presuppositional differences among disciplines distorts and trivializes those differences. If psychology simply explains its differences from social work as a conflict over status, degrees, and financial power, it disregards important information about the respective approaches each discipline takes in solving human problems and ameliorating human suffering. Nonetheless there has been a strong historical tendency to draw that very simplistic power assessment between the two professions.

Although lay people often treat each of the specialties as functionally equivalent, psychotherapists coming from different disciplines are not so easily categorized without a good knowledge of the professions. Social workers and psychologists frequently treat the same diagnostic categories in the same populations of clients. In this the two disciplines themselves may be somewhat culpable, using the term "psychotherapy" generically for both specialties. It is up to social workers and psychologists to gradually clarify for themselves and the general public that assumptions in social work and in psychology are different enough to produce distinctive stratagems.[3] This suggestion applies more strongly to clerics and medical doctors (including psychiatrists) whose disciplinary assumptions are even further removed from those of psychology.

SUGGESTIONS FOR LABELING DISCIPLINE APPROACHES

What is *not* needed in differentiating the therapy disciplines? We do not need to restrict the scope of any mental health specialty. To specify such a scope would be to enter into the territoriality and power debate that by now has grown stale. A deregulatory philosophy should prevail. Social work and psychology, for example, ought to be allowed by law and by mutual appreciation to address the same human problems and the same human populations.

What *is* needed are user-friendly labels to clearly differentiate the mental health specialties so that practitioners and the general public can identify and understand the distinctions. The term "psychotherapy" should be reserved for the work psychologists do. Historically and logically, psychology focuses uniquely on the operations of the mind as distinct from soul or body (*psycho* mind and *therapy* treatment). The mind is psychology's natural preoccupation and its unifying concern; when the mind is disordered, psychology offers treatment.

Social work has a different focus. It presupposes the reality of an organically dynamic group that is, in turn, expressed in its members' corporate behavior and experience. Morales and Sheafor (1980) say, "social work finds its strength and stability in its values—its beliefs in the worth of all people and in the possibility of *organizing society* so that each person can develop to his or her fullest potential." [emphasis added] (2) If social workers make use of psychological theories in therapy, and historically they have favored various forms of psychoanalysis, such theories should be in some measure integrated into meaningful sociological concepts to bring them into line with social work theory at a presuppositional level.[4] Accordingly, *social therapy* should be considered as a label for the social worker's specialty.

The clergy may be considered to engage in *spiritual counseling*. Psychiatrists practice *psychiatry*. No major public reeducation is needed, and no superiority of one specialty over another is implied or intended.

If the term "psychotherapy" is status-weighted from decades of territorial conflict, perhaps it ought to be jettisoned by all mental health specialties in the interest of clarity and mutual respect. It is noteworthy that in 1923 Karl Menninger proposed the term "orthophychics" to include generically the activity of all disciplines that offer services to treat personal human problems (Reisman 1966). Perhaps the time has come to follow Menninger's lead and to provide clearer labels for the various services offered to the public.

THE INDIVIDUALISM OF PSYCHOLOGY

Psychology has sometimes been criticized for its emphasis on individualism rather than on participation in social groups and joint efforts to solve common social problems. Perhaps the inevitable outcome of restricting the analysis of the human condition to the processes of individual minds is vacuous navel-gazing. That the services of a psychologist are fairly narrow in scope and focus may well be a valid criticism of psychology, but it does not demonstrate that such efforts are fruitless. They are only limited and need to be supplemented with insights from other disciplines. People have problems that are approachable as spiritual, medical, and social, as well as psychological. Social work obviously provides a needed balance to the narrower mental focus of psychology.

But it is not helpful to mistake major segments of social work theory or practice for psychological theory or practice. Maintaining this distinction does not reject social work, just as distinguishing between psychiatry and psychology does not reject the bodily side of human behavior and experience. A person is a member of a group whose corporate experience can be observed and examined independently of that member. This is helpful. But it is not psychology. An individual is more than internal thoughts and feelings—what we call the mind—but such thoughts and feelings may be validly designated as the domain of a separate discipline.

NOTES

1. Social work has also had its identity problems. An introductory social work textbook states, "[Social work's] particular scope and function are still only vaguely defined, its knowledge base has few irrefutable tenets, and the skills required of the social worker are in a constant state of flux. Yet social work finds its strength and stability in its values—its beliefs in the worth of all people and in the possibility of organizing society so that each person can develop to his or her fullest potential." (Morales and Sheafor 1980)

2. On a related question, two professors at the University of Washington School of Social Work argue that social workers should not engage in private practice because "despite the ever-widening domain and scope of the profession, social work practice has historically focused on: 1) improving or restoring social functioning of individuals, groups, and communities; 2) creating favorable socioenvironmental conditions. . . . and 3) matching resources with human needs." (Richey and Stevens 1992, 231) They feel that private practice is incompatible with these purposes.

3. Social work's distinctive ministration is illustrated by Morales and Sheafor (1980):

> It should be recognized that an individual needing help and the society offering it often view the purpose of social welfare differently, and the social worker and social agencies must mediate these differences. . . . The societal view might be described as an effort to improve society by returning the ill-functioning to full usefulness, to protect the status quo by helping deviants relate to the existing structure, and to serve as an expression of society's humanitarian efforts. It is evident that the social agency attempting to serve both the client and the society must somehow serve as the link between recipient and donor by providing service to the 'demanding recipient' with the sanction of the 'grudging donor.' (8)

4. It is perhaps risky to say so, but it appears that social work has been willing to accept within it whatever its popular identity might happen to

include. Of the four professions that engage in the work of psychotherapy, social work is the most eclectic (Jensen et al. 1990). In a survey of psychiatrists, psychologists, marriage and family therapists, and social workers, social workers reported using therapy methods derived from the four orientations of dynamic, systems, humanistic, and behavioral and cognitive theory—a greater breadth of borrowing than reported by the other three professions. The only one of these methods that is native to social work in the sense of applying organismic theory to the individual is family systems. Each of the others developed historically within psychology or psychiatry and has at least a limited primary focus on personal agency. Though it is unlikely to occur, it might be appropriate for social workers to acknowledge that, except when using family systems or similar theory in doing therapy, they are really functioning as psychologists doing traditional psychotherapy.

5

A Better Idea

*P*sychology needs to focus on a single, distinctive subject matter. For an array of historical reasons, its current subject matter has become confused with and sometimes subordinated to that of several other spheres of discourse and structured disciplines. This confusion and subordination distract from the central and difficult task of affirming and exploring *mind* in a culture whose worldview is primarily materialist and secondarily spiritist. In turn-of-the-twenty-first century Western culture, mind has become a weak and tertiary theme among psychologists. If psychology were not experiencing identity problems, the thesis here would hold little value.

However, many inside and outside the discipline sense these identity problems. If current dialogue within the largest organization of psychologists, the American Psychological Association, reflects prevalent attitudes, there is significant discontent. Questions of "what we are about" are repeatedly raised and discussed through commentary and letters in its monthly news organ, *The Monitor*, and in its primary journal, *The American Psychologist*.[1] Recent debate surrounding prescription privileges for psychologists has provided a context for examining identity and discipline boundary issues, and is illustrative of the current rhetoric. As background to this debate it should be noted that, at the time of writing, psychotropic medications could be prescribed legally only by physicians and certain other professionals.

Whether for or against granting prescription privileges to psychologists, those debating the issue tacitly appeal to available notions of what psychologists are and do. Generally, those more comfortable with psychology's current diffuse and fragmented self-understanding favor prescription privileges and those concerned about adding still another disparate responsibility to psychology's cultural mandate are opposed.

These alignments, however, do not always hold true. Joseph Pachman (1996), both a physician and a psychologist, argues that the psychologist's training and expertise in "cognitive-behavioral interventions and other types of psychotherapy" can be uniquely combined with medicine prescription to produce an overall outcome superior to what medication *or* psychotherapy alone would produce. This view appropriately values the essential psychologist's role as providing a meta-perspective from which to evaluate judiciously the potential efficacy of a medication within an overall intervention strategy.

In truth, it probably does not matter whether psychologists gain prescription privileges as long as physicalist intervention strategies by psychologists are subordinated to and pursued only in the service of genuinely psychological intervention strategies. After all, medication prescription is only one of many physicalist interventions presently available to psychologists: biofeedback, advice about diet and exercise, use of deep muscle relaxation for stress reduction, and behavioral (skill) training in such areas as touching while in the process of communicating.

If psychology's commitment to mind were solidly at the center of its identity, the availability of adjunctive physicalist interventions could present no serious threat. Such interventions would be supplementary to psychotherapy (as broadly defined) and not at all likely to replace it. It is only because of the preeminence and prestige of the medical profession, and of the deep philosophic materialism of our culture, that gaining the power of prescription privilege might constitute a threat to the survival of genuine psychology. In psychology's current state of fragmented and diffused identity, those privileges may prove to be too strong a temptation for psychology practitioners to emulate psychiatry in its forsaking of psychotherapy in favor of drug treatment.

It is in this sense that prescription privilege becomes a useful metaphor to represent all methodologies that are not in themselves intrinsically psychological but that are at times fruitfully included in psychological research and practice. These methodologies include social work and sociology. It is appropriate to study how minds respond and interact in various social roles and in group settings; it is not appropriate for the psychologist to consider people primarily as parts of a group when the group is understood as an organismic unit in which is played out an all-encompassing group dynamic. This understanding is the distinctive viewpoint of sociology. Social psychologists need to maintain their unique psychological perspective on such research.

Similarly, theological/religious beliefs, practices, and themes play an important part in the psychological life of some people. But, like prescription privileges and group dynamics theory, they are extrinsic to psychological inquiry, no matter how much value we may personally ascribe to them in the larger picture of human existence and destiny. Familiarity with theological systems and traditions may greatly aid in exploring psychological processes, but for the psychologist these systems must always remain external and tangential to the central exploratory task and must not be thought of as intrinsic parts. Predictably, this is not a welcome message to deeply religious people engaging in the psychological enterprise. To them it seems irreverent and inconsistent to *seriously* value sacred things (as I do) but insist that they are not central to the peculiar psychological task.

The most difficult alternate perspective to resist is not organismic social theory or a theological tradition. It is the enormously powerful materialist explanations offered by brain science. The promise of eventually reducing all psychological distress to an electrochemical circuitry malfunction and all therapy for this distress to pharmaceuticals, surgery, electroshock, or some rephasing of neural circuitry by behavioral reprogramming is difficult to resist. As a culture we are quite willing to expect breakthroughs concerning neural structures and neurotransmitters, but we are reluctant to expect such discoveries from new understandings of mental and motivational dynamics. This is true despite the exciting current work in cognitive science, including human information processing, stimulated by research in artificial intelligence.

So What Is Meant by "Mind"?—Revisited

Although cognitive science only implies a concept of mind, it definitely represents a significant statement of neomentalist theory. In a 1993 paper in the *American Psychologist*, brain scientist Roger Sperry states that recent cognitive research "represents a diametric turnaround in the centuries-old treatment of mind and consciousness in science."

Do minds really exist? This is part of a larger inquiry that philosophers label *ontology*, the question of being. It is easy for us to think that matter has being, but we are accustomed to considering mind as a sometimes useful illusion. Really, we think only matter matters. However, this doctrine is clearly a superstition in light of postmodern physics (Gilder 1996). Quantum theory in physics has shown that what we call matter can meaningfully be understood as wave-particles. Albert Einstein, Niels Bohr, and Werner Heisenberg showed us that it makes more sense to think of the universe as composed of particles of energy than of actual bits of matter (Kuhn 1996, 12). Gilder (1996) asserts that it is even reasonable to conceive of the quantum world "as a domain of ideas" which we can make "accessible to our minds. The quantum atom is largely an atom of information, a rich domain of information at the foundation of matter." (8) What we have thought of as the basic building block of matter may arguably be considered pieces of information to be processed by the mind.

Notwithstanding these interesting assertions by postmodern physicists, the ontological question of the existence of mind will not be resolved here. For the purposes of this book it is sufficient to establish that mind, more or less traditionally understood and adopted as a primary subject of our ordinary thought and of our academic/professional knowledge structures, has *just as much* legitimacy as do body and spirit. It is only through historical vagaries and fashions that one or another of these categories of reality is put away as useless or illegitimate. The irony is that psychologists may be the worst offenders.

But one other problem remains. From ancient times a strong reductionist desire has motivated humans to try to reduce everything to a single substance. This has been called the need for parsimony—to explain things in the simplest possible manner, using the fewest assumptions and the least complex explanations. This impulse is largely responsible for modern materialism as a universal explanatory domain for many people, just as spiritism is the monolithic explanatory principle in some cultures. That is, many in our culture believe that all human experiences are ultimately explicable as aspects of matter. Several generations ago there was a serious bid by radical mentalists to ascribe everything not to body or spirit but to mind, a bid well documented by Donald Meyer (1980). In an earlier century the philosopher Bishop Berkeley believed that the world of matter existed only because it was known and seen by the mind of God, making mind the preeminent reality (Titus 1953, 211).

The need for radical parsimony, the need to reduce everything to one substance, is another obstacle to the acceptance of mind as a genuine reality separate and autonomous from matter or spirit. This search for a single substance as a basis for all reality needs to be deliberately abandoned as postmodern science turns away from the ontological questions and asserts its appreciation for body, mind, spirit, and society as worthy and productive research foci. In theory, this pluralism should not be as difficult to achieve in postmodern science as it was in the modern era because the dividing line between matter and mind is no longer indubitably based on ontological distinctions. I believe, however, that it is still a helpful and important distinction to maintain.

Instead of searching for the fundamental reality that underlies all things (or assuming we know what it is), a functional, more language-analytic approach would be simply to agree that the time-honored categories of mind, body, spirit, and social organism are all equally meaningful. This could be considered the postmodern equivalent of a decision by modernist thinkers to treat as real each of these four domains.

But it would be a mistake to take this agreement to mean that the boundaries of disciplines traditionally clustered around the terms *body*, *mind*, *spirit*, and *society* can be heedlessly violated or ignored. That is the mistake of some contemporary psychology. Centuries of human observations and the knowledge stemming from them are contextualized within disciplinary categories. Imagine abandoning the "physical" in anatomy and physiology. Immediately this would be recognized as excessive, premature, and unhelpful. This concept becomes clearer as we think more about what it would mean to abandon the physical category. Although it is no longer possible for a quantum physicist to regard matter as fundamentally different from mere energy information, centuries of scientific findings and everyday observations about physical phenomena continue to be valid and useful to the biologist, chemist, physicist, and engineer. The physical sciences continue to be productive based on reality assumptions that have been supplemented (but not supplanted) by newer conceptions of matter/energy. Similarly, the idea of *mind* on which psychology was founded is at the center of an enormous volume of observations made in both clinical and informal settings. The validity and usefulness of these observations have not begun to be exhausted. But our great cultural skepticism about mind has threatened to paralyze its exploration even by those officially committed to the task, namely psychologists.

An interesting comparison can be made here. Those who wish to regain their religious faith are sometimes advised to proceed *as though* God exists. In doing so it is supposed that they will confirm their faith in a wholesome way. By analogy, psychologists might be well advised to proceed *as though* they believe minds exist; in that trust they will be astonished at the discoveries they will make in exploring human experience.

Am I just advocating another instance of academic conservatism, or even a form of academic fundamentalism? It does seem likely that the broad scientific exploration of the human condition will lead to the development of new disciplinary categories beyond and different from the current ones of medicine, psychology, theology, and sociology. This likely emergence of new category clusters might well parallel the emergence of medicine described in chapter 1 where the ancient splitting of medicine from priestly religious functions supported the emergence of medical science. As recently as the nineteenth century the scientific study of mind finally split from the older study of soul and body, so it is plausible that we have not yet seen the last of the evolution of this particular knowledge structure. But acknowledging that the development of human knowledge and the structures that contain it are never ending does not invalidate my point in this book.

Medicine as a discipline continues to flourish as both practitioners and patrons agree on its traditional focus and identity. Neither the public nor the functionaries of the religious enterprise are particularly unclear or ambivalent about what it entails. In contrast, psychology as a research and applied discipline was founded on the study of psyche, but because of the instability of its relative youth and perhaps because it developed simultaneously with the chaotic knowledge revolution/explosion of this century, psychology has become unsure and unsteady about its subject matter and its mandate. Because this was true of psychology, it was also inevitably true of its patrons and those it serves.

It is important to note that I am not proposing an exotic definition of *mind* in this book. The *New Merriam-Webster Dictionary* (1989) defines mind as "the part of an individual that feels, perceives, thinks, wills and especially reasons." This is a simple and adequate working definition. But it is one that has seemed surprisingly difficult to keep in focus over the more than 115 years of psychology's existence.

Reshaping Psychology Using the Better Idea

What practical difference would a focus on mind make in our everyday experience of psychology? First and most important, a psychology that takes mind seriously will be characterized by a peculiar and consistent standpoint. Beyond a change in standpoint there will be theoretical, curricular, methodological, and public relations implications as well. But underneath all of these will be a different standpoint, even a different attitude. This standpoint is best characterized as a settled confidence in the value of an unapologetic and rigorous scientific exploration of the mind. According to Webster's dictionary, that exploration will include a study of feeling, perceiving, thinking, and willing.

As with any perspective or standpoint, clues to its presence and character are sometimes subtle. Let me give one such clue. An examination of college-level textbooks used in introductory psychology courses reveals that the chapter presenting the brain and nervous system typically is titled something like the following: "The Biological Foundations of Psychology" (Feldman 1990), "The Biological Basis of Behavior" (Gleitman 1992; Lefton and Valvatne 1992; Smith 1993), or "Explanations of Behavior at the Level of the Nervous System" (Kalat 1993). Note the words "foundations" and "basis" in two of these titles, suggesting an explanatory bias that tends to make physicalist explanations primary. This obligatory brain chapter is usually located at the beginning of the book as one of the introductory chapters. Both the title and the positioning of this standard textbook chapter betray a bias and send a clear message that biology, the physical, is foundational and of prior importance.

So then it must be asked, does behavior have a *biological* basis that is more foundational, more basically explanatory, than that of *mind*? The truth is that we are prone in our culture to give an immediate affirmative answer to this question. Still, it is probable that some authors of these textbooks would deny that they believe this if they were given time to reflect. And publishers would likely object to deemphasizing the biology chapter by placing it toward the end of the book; they would claim it introduced a strange element into the textbook structure. If this general picture is true of textbooks in psychology, we must ask ourselves, what would be a reasonable alternative to textbooks' priorities as cited above? The answer is not to eliminate all biological considerations in the study of psychology, for such an elimination would be irresponsible. Instead, I am suggesting that taking mind seriously will lead to building a curriculum and structuring textbooks around truly psychological categories: feeling, perceiving, thinking, willing, and reason or the several modern equivalents of these categories that have emerged from respected lines of research. These psychological categories will not always conform exactly to the five topics given in Webster's dictionary, but they should show a clear affinity to those topics.

If this were done, how would peripheral biological, social, and spiritual information be presented to students of psychology? There are a number of possible ways. First, there are higher level undergraduate courses that deliberately interface psychology with other curricula in the same way that sociology interfaces with literature, astronomy with philosophy, or physics with biology. Courses in physiological psychology, social psychology, and spiritual therapy all seek to bridge the mind-body, mind-society, and mind-spirit gaps. These courses perform an important service. Within the psychology curriculum, psychology's relationship to other spheres of discourse can be clarified as their subject matter is studied.

Second, in an introductory psychology course, relevant supplementary information should be presented in a format that indicates its cognate but adjunctive relationship to psychology's primary subject matter. Textbooks for introductory courses in psychology are particularly crucial because they both shape and reflect current views of psychology's identity.

They partially determine what the next generation of psychologists will believe about their discipline as well as reveal what the current generation believes about it. The configuration of introductory psychology textbooks, of which there are approximately 200, has become fairly fixed as a matter of competitive marketing. Although differences in emphases and viewpoint exist among them, market factors dictate that considerable *uniformity* also exists.

How can the confounding of genuine psychological issues in introductory textbooks with nonpsychological cognate issues be addressed? Reformatting texts by placing chapters specifically on the brain, society, or spirituality in the book's concluding chapters, even in an appendix, is an option. Some books (e.g., Myers 1995) do this with chapters on statistical reasoning. It is doubtful that such a book would gain a substantial foothold in today's market, however.

The most natural way to solve this problem is to give this information *within the matrix* of genuine psychological theory and findings, clearly indicating its supplementary nature. The information would then be available to readers at the appropriate points in their studies and would also retain a specifically psychological focus. Even this strategy would not guarantee that psychology's distinctive concerns would be preserved. However, it would help avoid the implication that there is no jeopardy in moving heedlessly back and forth between psychology and the disciplines of brain science, theology, or sociology ignoring disciplinary boundaries. Nor would it imply that there simply *are* no significant disciplinary boundaries.

A few examples of the problem will be helpful. A bestselling psychology textbook is *Psychology* by David G. Myers (1995). In the chapter on emotion, the very first subtopic, "The Physiology of Emotion," occupies nearly five pages. The remainder of the chapter has these subtopics: "Expressing Emotion," "Experiencing Emotion," and "Theories of Emotion." A close look at all four of these subtopics is warranted. Whether intentionally or not, this sequence gives the impression that emotion is principally a physical phenomenon that may be expressed only incidentally. Although Myers's intent may be to address the less important physiological aspect of emotion early, the history of research on emotion contains a strong biological focus, and Myers's chapter reflects this construct of psychology's identity.[2]

A textbook approach like this makes good sense from a physicalist viewpoint, but in my view it does not give *primary* place to that which is distinctly psychological in the study of emotion. The goal is to find a structure for a chapter on emotion that clearly conveys a distinctively psychological standpoint. How can this be done?

First, it should be noted that when particular topics about emotion are addressed—interpreting facial expressions, analyzing fear and anger, understanding happiness—much of the research can stand alone, independent of physiology or biology. A good example is the feel-good, do-good phenomenon originally discovered by Salovey (1990). This phenomenon suggests that people who are happy have a greater willingness to help others. There are doubtless physiological states peculiar to these psychological phenomena, but a description of them is not needed, nor would it add anything to the findings as presented.

What *is* true of the feel-good, do-good phenomenon applies to a number of other findings in the area of emotion. For example, there is no need to specify the *biology* of happiness (brain endorphins, adequate serotonin, etc.) in order to explore the distinctly psychological finding that dramatically negative and dramatically positive events have only temporary effects on happiness level (Myers 1995, 448). It is this kind of research conclusion that is at the core of psychology.

Examples from one more psychological area will suffice. The area of therapy efficacy research is of interest to both academic and practicing psychologists. The metastudies of psychotherapy effectiveness are eminently appropriate to psychology's central focus and can be and usually are done in a way that is not bolstered by information from the medical, spiritual, or social domains (Strupp and Howard 1992). The popular design of comparing psychotherapy with pharmacotherapy is instructive and important, but a design that does not happen to include any somatic treatment is statistically just as sound. The latter design would be a thoroughly psychological study just as the former should be regarded as adjunctive and valuable to psychology's central concern. Currently, the reverse is the case: A comparison of psychopharmical effects with psychotherapy is considered to be a quintessentially psychological study.

Today popular interest in drug treatment versus psychotherapy is high. The reason is simple: The trust that dialogue between therapist and client can significantly alter serious behavior disorders has publicly eroded. This is even true, to some extent, within the ranks of psychologists. The debate has centered instead on trying to prove that psychotherapy can duplicate or exceed the effects of medications.

A researcher who holds a consistently psychological perspective proceeds on the *assumption* of the efficacy of psychotherapy with the only questions to be investigated having to do with *what kinds* of therapy are appropriate under which conditions and with which problems/clients. There is a venerable tradition of such studies by psychologically minded researchers. To again cite Myers's (1995) general psychology textbook, the chapter on therapy is thirty-three pages long and the somatic therapies are restricted to an admirable five pages (15 percent). This is appropriate for a general psychology textbook, although it could be argued that even those five pages could be placed in the book's appendix.

This brief exploration of curriculum and textbooks illustrates the practical complexity of attempting to define psychology more circumspectly. There are many other illustrative artifacts that reflect and support an excessively diffused disciplinary identity. It will require determination and effort for psychology to extricate itself from this plight.

Two Recent "Freud" Figures Who Reintroduce Mind

In chapter 3, I explored the irony that a physician, Sigmund Freud, rather than a professional psychologist, provided early in psychology's history the single most enduring psychological system that embraces mind. Although it has been argued that Freud's system can ultimately be reduced to biology, I contend that an irreducible concept of mind may be found even in the context of his materialist determinism, with which *mind* is tacitly at odds. It took the new Freudians to show that Freud's understanding of mind can stand by itself without biological underpinnings.[3]

Freud established a robust precedent for latter-day reformers, speaking powerfully from outside psychology, to effectively address the practical need for mentalism. Just as with Freud, these recent reform movements typically begin on the outer fringes of psychology and gradually work their way into its center, meeting a need that even they do not completely appreciate. At the end of the twentieth century two figures who promise to perform that function are Stephen Covey and M. Scott Peck—a business management seminar leader and a psychiatrist. Let us consider first the enormous popular appeal of Stephen Covey. With others in the business management seminar circuit, Covey seems destined to shape the identity of psychology, a process that has already begun.

A psychologist coming to Covey's best-selling book, *The Seven Habits of Highly Effective People* (1989), will be struck immediately by how little in it is new. A typical first response might be, "What is the big fuss about? We have known all of these principles for decades." Some psychologists may even experience hints of jealousy, as though their territory has been violated. In truth, most of Covey's assertions have been borrowed from research findings in psychology and tailored for business by "highly effective people." So then, what is his irresistible innovation?

The book's subtitle, "Restoring the Character Ethic," lends a clue. It is a book about character, psychology, and business. But character assumes and implies some locus, some repository in which character can dwell. It cannot meaningfully exist in the abstract. Character cannot exist apart from some comprehensive mental structure that goes well beyond a list of neuromechanical functions. Not professing to be a psychologist, Covey simply ignores and thereby circumvents the philosophical problems attendant on establishing a scientific basis for character, not the least of which is the prior need for self or mind. Covey and his followers assume that mind and character are self-evident features of human experience that cannot be neglected with impunity. They are right.

This national bestseller identifies three selected habits that may help illustrate the compelling thirst for a mentalist framework. The first habit says "Be proactive." Proactivity is in contrast to reactivity, and reactivity has historically been at the essence of the mechanistic "scientific" paradigm in psychology. Thus *proactivity* strikes at the core of mechanism, a point that earlier was argued articulately by such psychological theorists as D.A. Lieberman (1979), George Miller (1962), and Abraham Maslow (1968). Empowering an individual to change his/her life presupposes a belief in proactivity. In fact, as psychologist Julian Rotter's (1966) research shows, the more one believes in self-determination, the more the prophesy of self-determination comes true. However, traditional psychology, disbelieving in mind, finds itself in a position of having to assert that fact, clearly supported by research, simultaneously denying that there is really any such thing as self-determination. Ordinary people and intuitive psychologists sense that there is something very wrong with this doubletalk.

Covey's fourth habit states, "Think win/win." Here readers are exhorted to avoid assuming that their advantage must come at the expense of another's disadvantage. Sometimes that trade-off occurs, but not always. But notice that to decide to "think win/win," one must engage in a metacognition, a top-down monitoring of lower psychological/emotional functions. To "think win/win" one must simultaneously attend to both the tactics required to accomplish a goal (for example, winning an account) and the more metacognitive issue of accomplishing the goal in a synergistic rather than combative mode. Covey correctly presumes that his readership is fully capable of juggling several levels of complex cognition, and his challenge to them has been met with grateful enthusiasm on their part. It is as though a psychologically literate writer has, through his trust in them, finally permitted them what their best intuitions have always known themselves capable of. In return, they have rewarded him richly.

My last example is Covey's seventh habit, "Sharpen the saw," wherein he exhorts his readers to renew regularly the quality of their lives, physically, socially, spiritually, and mentally. What is noteworthy is the use Covey makes of these four traditional dimensions of human life and experience. Covey wisely omits philosophical arguments about which dimension(s) among the four may be more real and which may be less real. Instead, he implies his ingenuous assumption of their parity. This comes as an enormous relief to readers who have secretly struggled, depending partly on their philosophical stances, with self-criticism for their ignorance in thinking in such naive traditional categories.

For my part, I do not want to dismiss as irrelevant the ontological questions inevitably raised by this grouping of physical, spiritual, mental, and social dimensions of life experience. On the contrary, I welcome the critical philosophical examination of this issue as part of the current debate about psychology's identity because I believe such an examination will challenge the prevailing assumption that the physical, and perhaps the spiritual, dimension(s) has an ontologically superior status compared to the mental. The force of this challenge will come both from the pervasively weakened trustworthiness of ontological analysis in postmodern thought and from arguments in favor of the comparative reality of mind as I have tried to present them in this book.

It is noteworthy that Covey has forcefully made his points about certain mental habits without much appeal to medical findings, religious truths, or social constructs. He has done this by almost completely staying within the realm of mind, by reminding educated people at the end of the 1990s of what they have known intuitively: the sheer power of a focused and motivated mind. This is precisely psychology's message, one that psychology is equipped by decades of research to promote and explain. In this way, we are called back by a marginal figure to our peculiar cultural mandate.

In Stephen Covey we observe a popular spokesperson slightly beyond the margins of academic psychology and within the community of motivational seminars speaking on behalf of a psychology of mind. Simultaneously, from within psychiatry, a spokesperson with Freud-like autonomy who holds promise of performing the same function has emerged. His name is M. Scott Peck. In contrast to mainstream psychiatry, Peck deliberately rejects the physicalist (brain science) reductionism of mind. This curious rejection, together with his prestigious Harvard Medical School position, makes him stand out among psychiatrists as dramatically distinctive. Peck (1983) not only tacitly acknowledges mind but also acknowledges spirit and spiritual issues.

Because he is regrettably unclear in distinguishing the several spheres of discourse, Peck violates a central contention of this book. Currently, he moves from one sphere to another, giving little or no cue that he is doing so. However, he is noteworthy in acknowledging, with Covey, the conceptual standing of moral, spiritual, mental, and social domains as equal with the physical. This alone is enough to win for him public and professional attention. He makes these important affirmations in his first best-selling volume, *The Road Less Traveled* (1979). With the popularity of his first book, Peck had a unique opportunity to make an effective, sustained case for mind, distinct from body or spirit, as a legitimate focus of both research and therapy. Making such a case would have been an invaluable service to psychological science. But he failed to make it. Having escaped physicalist reductionism, he shortly succumbed to the opposite temptation by falling into a spiritualist reductionism in some of his writings. In

1983, he wrote *People of the Lie: The Hope for Healing Human Evil*, an amalgam of theology and existentialist psychology, mostly anecdotal in form. In the book, Peck takes up such questions as the existence of Satan and the nature of evil without adequately acknowledging that his credentials as a medical doctor and psychiatrist give him no particular expertise to address these topics. In this way, I believe he largely forfeits his chance to strengthen psychological science.

I say "largely forfeits" because, to be fair to Peck, the overall effect of someone who is perceived as a representative of mainstream psychiatry writing ingenuously about theological topics is probably supportive of this book's thesis. The reason for that is, despite the blurring of disciplinary boundaries, he does defy the prevailing physicalist assumptions that were especially important in the early 1980s. Recall Carl Jung's statement that first psychology lost its soul and then it lost its mind; similarly, it is harder to deny mind if one begins by affirming soul. And affirm soul is exactly what Peck does in *The People of the Lie*. Not entirely oblivious to the problems of mixing concepts from several distinct disciplines, Peck notes some "dangers of a psychology of evil" in his final chapter.

Although Peck does not affirm mind per se, he does repeatedly leap into the spiritual domain and, in the process, mingles theological and psychological terms. Happily, in so doing, he creates a "space" for the domain of mind—a step forward. This is the second most valuable service he could render to psychology, having failed to remain steadfastly within a nonphysicalist and nonspiritist mental sphere of discourse.

In addition to Covey and Peck, there are other well-respected or popular writers not found in the mainstream of psychology who have issued serious calls to reconsider mind, or who, more accurately, have never stopped believing in mind. An example is Bill Moyers in his book *Healing and the Mind* (1993), promoted by booksellers under the telling slogan, "Mind over Matter."

Psychology's Future

The uniform theme of this book has been the renewal of psychology by reaffirming the original elements of identity it had when it emerged as a truly new science at the end of the nineteenth century. For all of its shortcomings, the structuralism of Titchener and especially that of Wundt focused on mind, an entity whose existence was simply assumed by all (Murray 1988). But the dual impact of a culturally pervasive material- ism—the belief in matter as the *only* reality—together, ironically, with a general postmodern skepticism regarding ontology—the loss of our belief that *any* reality can be really established—seriously undercut psychology's essential foundation as a science of the mind. To survive, psychology temporarily took several disguised identities to camouflage its culturally unacceptable nature. Novices trained during this midcentury period some- times had difficulty discerning psychology's unique mandate, although they often sensed that the science was the closest to their felt interest. It confused them with many false promises and led them on many wild- goose chases.

During this period, however, some theorists, researchers, academics, clinicians, and psychology practitioners quietly maintained a steady focus on psychology's peculiar mandate. As this book comes to an end, a brief survey of these resolute psychologists and their programs is in order as an optimistic and hopeful conclusion to an otherwise critical exposition. It is my intention to say what is right with psychology in its current state, and why it is still true that there is no other discipline equipped to perform psychology's unique service.

A good place to start is to note psychology's reasonably hospitable posture toward several developmental theorists in the Kantian philosoph- ical tradition, including Noam Chomsky (1972), Erik Erikson (1963), Lawrence Kohlberg (1984), and Jean Piaget (1972). All four were theorists who asserted that every neonate is born already possessing the rudiments of mind, and that the unfolding of genetic mental potential, whether in the area of cognitive, social, linguistic, or moral development, takes place in an orderly manner according to a set sequence of critical periods or stages. In this view, mind does not grow primarily as a consequence of enculturation or conditioning from the outside. Rather, it grows from the inside, provided that the social environment gives minimally nurturing conditions. In the wake of these ontogenic theorists are many distin- guished researchers who also swim valiantly against the British and Amer- ican *tabula rasa* empiricist mainstream.

Another natural locus in psychology where the precious gem of mind is preserved and guarded is personality theory. Like the developmentalists, personality theorists as a group were not immediately welcomed into the psychology fold. But through the persistence of giants like Gordon Allport (1961), books were written, courses offered, and degrees granted in the personality subfield and, although it still does not enjoy a prominent place in psychology, personality theory has become a permanent fixture of the psychological curriculum. Some names to be noted here are Carl Jung (1953), George Kelly (1955), Abraham Maslow (1968), Henry Murray (1938), and Carl Rogers (1961).

Two subfields that are auxiliary to personality theory are also predictably welcoming to mind, namely, psychological disorders and psychotherapy. Not *all* who do research in these areas acknowledge mind, but it is difficult (though not impossible) to understand most psychological disorders without reference to some ordinary language form of consciousness. Most of the criteria found in the *Diagnostic and Statistical Manual of the American Psychiatric Association—IV* (1994) have one or more components that rely on subjective qualitative reporting of an affective/cognitive state by the client. For the diagnosis of a Major Depressive Episode, for example, subjective reporting of sadness, diminished pleasure in activities, feelings of worthlessness and guilt, diminished ability to think, and recurrent thoughts of death can all be diagnostic markers. An effective diagnosis of this and many other disorders would be virtually impossible without access to these reports. It is possible to take a behaviorist view that such reports are "verbal behaviors" that can be analyzed without assuming consciousness, as can any other objective behaviors, but this is an awkward construction, difficult to sustain in practice. Psychodiagnosticians are justifiably more inclined simply to take such reports at face value using precise, but commonsense, meanings.

Likewise, psychotherapy theory and practice have often tacitly assumed mind except in its more deliberately behavioristic forms. The dynamic therapies derived from psychoanalysis assume a subconscious mind that is purposeful and functionally integrated even though not easily accessible. Similarly, the Gestalt therapies seek to help clients to discover and explore their moment-by-moment experience. Cognitive therapies, despite eschewing a return to true mentalism, aim at examining dysfunctional ways of cognitively constructing oneself and one's world with the hope of restructuring that viewpoint into a healthier one. All of these therapies presuppose what is usually and meaningfully meant by *mind*.

Cognitive therapy leads us to think broadly about the renewed interest in the theory of cognition and, consequently, of modern cognitive psychology as a natural home for mind. Even though cognitive theorists in psychology have been careful to avoid a simplistic return to mentalism, whether it is found in nineteenth-century psychology or some popular "commonsense" form, there are some studies of learning, memory, thinking, and language that do not expend much effort protesting or denying mind as it inevitably is implied between the lines.[4]

The caution to avoid espousing a naive version of mentalism is reminiscent of some motivational theorists in the 1960s and 1970s who were inclined to affirm some version of instinct theory but who were also painfully aware of the abuse to which the idea of instinct had been subjected by William McDougall (1912) at the beginning of the century. The result of their caution was that they bent over backwards to avoid the term "instinct" and overdocumented any evidence for whatever instinctive phenomenon they postulated. An excellent example of this is attachment theory in infants as developed by Ainsworth (1973) and others, where the affinity to instinct theory is treated with utmost discretion. Since history tends to repeat itself, a similar level of caution is currently evident among cognitive psychologists as they valiantly struggle to avoid using language that suggests naive belief in mind lest they be thought to superstitiously accede to an anachronistic fiction. It *is* a fiction that they correctly sense can lead to a lazy short-circuiting of progress on specifying in detail how cognition theoretically works. An excellent example of such progress is the work of John Anderson (1996) cited earlier.

But there *are* cognitive psychologists who were, and are, willing to face the issue squarely and take a solid stand for mind. In a 1979 *American Psychologist* article, T. Natsoulas documented in detail the return of the topic of consciousness in the literature of psychology. This was followed in the same journal by a piece by D. A. Lieberman titled "Behaviorism and the Mind: A (Limited) Call for a Return to Introspection." Both of these articles are daring, even radical, as perhaps is permitted only to certain mature theorists and journals of status within psychology. The articles audaciously connect the new cognitive movement with more ordinary-language mind concerns and, in so doing, call psychology back to its central mandate.

The establishing of a Center for Cognitive Studies at Harvard University by George Miller and Jerome Bruner represents a similar watershed statement. According to Schultz and Schultz (1996), Miller "saw the movement as more evolutionary than revolutionary and believed it was a return to a common sense psychology, one that recognized and affirmed that psychology dealt with mental life as well as behavior." (450) It is unlikely that in those pioneering years at the Center Miller could have plausibly identified mind as the focus of study (as contrasted with an accepted list of specific cognitive processes as the stated foci of research). But no great logical leap is required for us to so construe its focus.

This thumbnail sketch of the courageous founding of cognitive psychology would not be complete without mentioning Ulric Neisser, sometimes regarded as its father. His books (1967, 1976) define the basic perspective of cognitive psychology and later express his dissatisfaction with the way it developed. His criticisms center on its artificiality and detachment from reality. Even though, as with Miller and Bruner, he never formally identified mind as the proper focus of psychological science, it is not hard now to construe his disappointment as an understandable response to a perceived failure by cognitive psychology to address real problems of life in a way consistent with acknowledgment of the human mind.

One of the more cogent criticisms of cognitive psychology in its current form is that its emphasis on information processing and the computer metaphor makes it too "heady," tending to leave out motivational and affective factors historically important to psychology as a discipline. An idea ignored in the older cognitive perspective can be added to this deficiency. It is illustrated by a new interest in something like volition that has recently appeared on the scene in the work of George Howard (1996) and his associates.

I believe that a deliberate focus on mind as psychology's subject matter will nicely counterbalance the deficiency of cognitive science. Mind includes all that we usually include within cognition *as well as* notions of drive, feeling, and volition. When I "make up my mind" to do something, I am thinking, choosing, and wanting to do that thing. No other term can bear the linguistic weight implied by mind. It is ideal now, as it has always been, for psychology's purposes. We must be always vigilant to the ubiquitous danger of using mind as a pseudo-explanation, a kind of *deus ex machina* that magically explains everything instantly.

A Concluding Note

A main theme of this book has emphasized that an identity search, whether by an adolescent individual or by an academic discipline, is just as dependent on what is consciously *excluded* as on what is included. An "identity-achieved" young adult, according to James Marcia (1980), can tell us in the realm of ideology what she does not believe along with what she does. Similarly, her vocational choice precludes a multitude of other possibilities. Accepting a particular gender role definition means that she foregoes defining herself in a whole array of other available ways. These exclusions considered within the context of an identity search are not considered narrow-mindedness or bigotry, but, on the contrary, are considered healthy human development.

Virtually everyone believes in the existence of the body, even if some ontological philosophers might call it into question. Many also believe in the existence of spirit, coming from one or another religious or quasi-religious perspective, either Western or Eastern. Most even believe in mind—with the ironic exception of psychologists who have managed to talk themselves out of it. But within a segment of the psychology community that may, however, be considered marginal, the thirst for serious consideration of the mind is seen in the popularity of Scott Peck, Stephen Covey, Bill Moyers, Robert Schuller, and other popular writers.

These writers may be seen as writing for a naive and technically uninformed public. It is true that they are writing for nonprofessionals, but they are also making an important theoretical statement to the psychological community. Psychology needs to stake its claim again to the territory once occupied by Wundt, Fechner, Brentano, and Freud. In so doing, it will rediscover and reclaim its true identity.

At places in this book, it may have seemed that the major impulse for the return to mind was a pragmatic one—either because it is popular outside psychology or because it will help us to define our peculiar social mandate in sharper contrast to other natural and social scientists or service professionals. These pragmatic concerns are important; however, it is not from these concerns that I have written. Rather, I have written the book because I am a true believer in mind.

In what sense it should turn out that mind "exists" is somewhat a secondary consideration for me, provided only that its existence is considered to have no *lesser* reality than body or spirit. That is crucial to psychology's continuing well-being.

NOTES

1. It may seem paradoxical, but I would agree with Kenneth Gergin et al. (1996), who write, "looking from the bridge between East and West . . . I believe we must press toward an appreciation of differing philosophic traditions and in the direction of psychology's interculturation. Continuous consideration of the varied epistemological and metapsychological assumptions underlying and fertilizing mainstream psychology is necessary to soften the discipline's rigid boundaries." (501) However, I contend that the "rigid boundaries" of mainstream American psychology have largely *excluded* serious consideration of mind for a good portion of its recent history. We may find that other cultures are much more open to serious consideration of mind.

2. This is a vastly different publishing scenario from 1890, when William James published his two-volume text that became the standard work used to teach psychology.

3. Again, a rather sophisticated emergentism is able to accommodate a form of materialism that takes mind seriously, but I believe most psychologists do not hold this view.

4. A recent ingenious, rigorous, and significant analysis of human cognition by John R. Anderson (1996) cannot avoid tacit reference to mind. After showing that an interaction of procedural and declarative knowledge units enables people to combine information in a way that is optimal for problem solving, he notes that "although Bayesian inference is nonintuitive and often people's conscious judgments do not accord with it (even when their behavior does . . .), it is really a very simple mechanism. Thus, we achieve great adaptiveness in

knowledge deployment by simple statistical inference." (364) His reference to intuition and "people's conscious judgments" suggest a sector of cognition that is logically (or at least linguistically) separable from the results of his analysis. Why is it that a small portion of cognition inevitably seems to lie outside every analysis?

Works Cited

Ainsworth, M.D.S. 1973. The development of infant-mother attachment. In B. Caldwell & Ricciuti (Eds.), *Review of child development research* (Vol. 3). Chicago: University of Chicago Press.

Allport, G. 1961. *Pattern and growth in personality.* New York: Holt.

Altman, I. 1987. Centripetal and centrifugal trends in psychology. *American Psychologist, 42,* 1058–1069.

Anderson, John R. 1996. ACT: a simple theory of complex cognition. *American Psychologist, 51,* 355–365.

Bandura, Albert. 1986. *Social foundation of thought and action: a social-cognitive theory.* Englewood Cliffs, NY: Prentice-Hall.

Beers, Clifford. 1908. *A mind that found itself.* New York: Longmans, Green.

Benassi, V.A., Sweeney, P.D., and Dufour, C.L. 1988. Is there a relation between locus of control orientation and depression? *Journal of Abnormal Psychology, 97,* 357–367.

Berkouwer, G.C. 1962. *Man: the image of God.* Grand Rapids: Wm B. Eerdmans.

Bernstein, Richard J. 1983. *Beyond objectivism and relativism: science, hermeneutics, and praxis.* Philadelphia: University of Pennsylvania Press.

Boring, Edwin. 1950. *A history of experimental psychology* (2nd ed.). New York: The Century Co.

Britannica, The New Encyclopedia 1991 (15th ed.). London: Encyclopedia Britannica, Inc.

Buber, Martin. 1958. *I and Thou* (2nd ed.). New York: Charles Scribner's Sons.

Chomsky, Noam. 1972. *Language and mind.* New York: Harcourt Brace Jovanovich.

Cohen, Louis. 1992. The academic department. In Freedman (Ed.) *History of psychotherapy: a century of change.* Washington, DC: American Psychological Association.

Covey, Stephen R. 1989. *The seven habits of highly effective people.* New York: Simon and Shuster.

DeAngelis, T. 1989. Suit opens doors to analysis training. *The APA Monitor, 20,* 16.

Diagnostic manual of the American Psychiatric Association—IV. 1994. Washington, DC: American Psychiatric Association.

Dobson, J. 1974. *Hide and seek.* Old Tappan, NJ: Revell.

Dooyeweerd, Herman. 1953. *A new critique of theoretical thought.* Amsterdam: H.J. Paris.

Duggan, J.P., and Booth, D.A. 1986. Obesity, overeating and rapid gastric emptying in rats with ventromedial hypothalamic lesions. *Science, 231,* 609–611.

Eagle, Morris N., and David L. Wolitzky. 1992. Psychoanalytic theories of psychotherapy. In Freedheim, Donald K. (Ed.) *History of psychotherapy: a century of change.* Washington, DC: American Psychological Association.

Elkin, I., Shea, M.T., Watkins, J.T., Imber, S.D., Sotsky, S.M., Collins, J.F., Glass, D.R., Pilkonis, P.A., Leber, W.R., Docherty, J.P., Fiester, S.J., and Parloff, M.B. 1989. National Institute of Mental Health Treatment of Depression Collaborative Research Program. *Archives of General Psychiatry, 46,* 971–982.

Erikson, Erik. 1963. *Childhood and society.* New York: Norton.

Evans, C. Stephen. 1989. *Wisdom and humanness in psychology.* Grand Rapids, MI: Baker.

Fechner, G. 1860/1966. *Elements of psychophysics.* New York: Holt, Rinehart and Winston.

Feldman, Robert S. 1990. *Understanding psychology* (2nd ed.). New York: McGraw-Hill Publishing Co.

Foucault, M. 1988. The political technologies of individuals. In L. Martin, H. Gutman, and P. Hutton (Eds.). *Technologies of the self—a seminar with Michel Foucault.* Amherst: University of Massachusetts Press.

Freedheim, Donald K. (Ed.) 1992. *History of psychotherapy: a century of change.* Washington, DC: American Psychological Association.

Freud, Sigmund. 1953–1974. All works mentioned in the text will be found in J. Strachey (Ed.) *The complete psychological works of Sigmund Freud* (24 vols.). London: Hogarth Press and the Institute of Psychoanalysis.

Freud, S. 1905/1953. *Three essays on the theory of sexuality.* In J. Strachey, op. cit.

Freud, S. 1927/1961. *The future of an illusion.* In J. Strachey, op. cit.

Gergin, Kenneth. 1985. The social constructionism movement in modern psychology. *American Psychologist, 40,* 266–275.

Gergin, Kenneth, Aydan Gulerce, Andrew Lock, and Girishwar Misra. 1996. Psychological science in cultural context. *American Psychologist, 51,* 496–503.

Gilder, George. 1996. The materialist superstition. *The Intercollegiate Review, 31,* (2), 6–14.

Glass, C. and Arnkoff, D. 1992. Behavior therapy. In Freedheim, Donald K. (Ed.) *History of psychotherapy: a century of change.* Washington, DC: American Psychological Association.

Gleitman, Henry. 1992. *Basic psychology* (3rd ed.). New York: W.W. Norton and Co.

Grossman, Reinhardt. 1992. *The Existence of the world: an introduction to ontology.* London: Routledge.

Harre, R. 1984. *Personal being: a theory for individual psychology.* Cambridge, MA: Harvard University Press.

Hawking, Stephen W. 1993. *A brief history of time.* New York: Bantam Doubleday.

Hilgard, Ernest R. 1987. *Psychology in America: a historical survey.* New York: Harcourt Brace Jovanovich.

Horney, K. 1937. *The neurotic personality of our time.* New York: Norton.

Howard, George. 1996. *Understanding human nature.* Academic Press.

Hull, Clark L. 1952. *A behavior system.* New Haven, CT: Yale University Press.

Iacono, W.G., and Grove, W.M. 1993. Schizophrenia reviewed: toward an integrative genetic model. *Psychological Science, 4,* 273–276.

James, William. 1958. *The varieties of religious experience.* New York: New American Library.

Jensen, J.P., Bergin, A.E,, and Greaves, D.W. 1990. The meaning of eclecticism: new survey and analysis of components. *Professional psychology: research and practice, 21,* 124–130.

Jung, C.J. 1916. *The psychology of the unconscious.* (B.M. Hinkle, trans.). New York: Moffat, Yard.

Jung, C.J. 1953. *Two essays on analytical psychology.* New York: Pantheon.

Kalat, James W. 1993. *Introduction to psychology* (3rd ed.). Pacific Grove, CA: Brooks/Cole.

Kelly, George A. 1955. *The psychology of personal constructs.* New York: Norton.

Keys, A., Brozek, J., Henschel, A., Mickelsen, O., and Taylor, H.L. 1950. *The biology of human starvation.* Minneapolis: University of Minnesota Press.

Kohlberg, Lawrence. 1984. *The psychology of moral development: essays on moral development.* (Vol. II) San Francisco: Harper and Row.

Kuhn, Thomas S. 1996. *The structure of scientific revolutions* (3rd ed.). Chicago: University of Chicago Press.

Lazarus, A.A. 1991. Does chaos prevail? an exchange on technical eclecticism and assimilative integration. *Journal of Psychotherapy Integration, 1,* 143–158.

Lefton, Lester A., and Valvatne, Laura. 1992. *Mastering psychology* (4th ed.). Boston: Allyn and Bacon.

LeVay, Simon. 1991. A difference in hypothalamic structure between heterosexual and homosexual men. *Science, 253,* 1034–1037.

Lieberman, D.A. 1979. Behaviorism and the mind: a (limited) call for a return to introspection. *American Psychologist, 34,* 319–333.

Loeb, J. 1918. *Forced movements, tropisms, and animal conduct.* Philadelphia: Lippincott.

MacCorquodale, K., and Meehl, P.E. 1948. On a distinction between hypothetical constructs and intervening variables. *Psychological Review, 55,* 95–107.

McDougall, William. 1912. *Psychology: the study of behavior.* London: Oxford University Press.

Marx, Karl, and Engels, Friedrich 1848/1967. *The Communist manifesto.* New York: Washington Square Press.

Mandler, George. 1984. *Mind and body: psychology of emotion and stress.* New York: W.W. Norton and Co.

Marcia, James. 1980. Identity in adolescence. In J. Adelson (Ed.). *Handbook of adolescent psychology.* New York: Wiley.

Maslow, A.H. 1968. *Toward a psychology of being.* (2nd ed.). New York: Van Nostrand Reinhold.

Maslow, A. H. 1979. *The journals of Abraham Maslow* (Vols. 1–2; R.J. Lowry, Ed.). Menlo Park, CA: International Study Project.

May, Rollo. 1967. Existential psychology. In T. Millon (Ed.). *Theories of psychopathology.* Philadelphia: Saunders.

Menninger, Karl. 1988. *Whatever became of sin?* New York: Bantam Books.

Meyer, Donald. 1980. *Positive thinkers: religion as pop psychology from Mary Baker Eddy to Oral Roberts* (2nd ed.). New York: Pantheon Books.

Miller, George A. 1962. *Psychology: the science of mental life.* New York: Harper & Row.

Morales, Armando, and Sheafor, Bradford. 1980. *Social work: a profession of many faces.* (2nd ed.). Boston: Allyn and Bacon, Inc.

Moyers, Bill D. 1993. *Healing and the mind.* New York: Doubleday.

Murray, David J. 1988. *A history of Western psychology.* (2nd ed.). Englewood Cliffs, NJ: Prentice Hall.

Murray, Henry A. 1938. *Explorations in personality.* New York: Oxford University Press.

Myers, David G. 1995. *Psychology.* (4th ed.). New York: Worth Publishers.

Natsoulas, T. 1979. Concerning "residual subjectivity." *The American Psychologist, 34,* 640–642.

Neisser, U. 1967. *Cognitive psychology.* New York: Appleton-Century-Crofts.

Neisser, U. 1976. *Cognition and reality.* San Francisco: W. H. Freeman.

The New Merriam-Webster Dictionary 1989. Springfield, MA: Merriam-Webster, Inc.

Pachman, Joseph S. 1996. The dawn of a revolution in mental health. *American Psychologist, 51,* 213–215.

Peale, N.V. 1953. *The power of positive thinking.* New York: Prentice-Hall.

Peck, M. Scott. 1979. *The road less traveled.* New York: Simon and Schuster.

Peck, M. Scott. 1983. *People of the lie.* New York: Simon and Schuster.

Piaget, Jean. 1972. Intellectual evolution from adolescence to adulthood. *Human Development, 15,* 1–12.

Piaget, Jean. 1977. *The development of thought: equilibration of cognitive structure.* New York: Viking.

Polanyi, Michael. 1958. *Personal knowledge: towards a post-critical philosophy.* London: Routledge & Kegan Paul.

Popper, Karl. 1959. *The logic of scientific discovery.* New York: Basic Books.

Reisman, J.M. 1966. *The development of clinical psychology.* New York: Appleton-Century-Crofts.

Richey, Cheryl, and Stevens, Gail. 1992. Is private practice a proper form of social work? In Gambril, E., and Pruger, R. (Eds.). Controversial issues in social work. Boston: Allyn and Bacon.

Riess, Bernard F. 1992. Postdoctoral training: toward professionalism. In Donald K. Freedheim (Ed.). *History of psychotherapy: a century of change.* Washington, DC: American Psychological Association.

Rogers, Carl. 1961. *On becoming a person*. Boston: Houghton Mifflin.

Rogers, Carl. 1967. Carl R. Rogers. In Boring, E.G., and Gardner Lindsey (Eds.). *A history of psychology in autobiography* (Vol. 5). New York: Appleton-Century-Crofts.

Rosenbaum, M., Lakin, M., and Roback, H. 1992. Psychotherapy in groups. In Donald K. Freedheim (Ed.). *History of psychotherapy: a century of change*. Washington, DC: American Psychological Association.

Rotter, Julian. 1966. Generalized expectancies for internal versus external control of reinforcement. *Psychological monographs*, 80 (609) (entire issue).

Rushton, J.P. 1989. Genetic similarity, human altruism, and group selection. *Behavioral and brain sciences, 12*, 503–559.

Rychlak, Joseph F. 1988. *The psychology of rigorous humanism* (2nd ed.). New York: New York University Press.

Rychlak, J.F. 1993. A suggested principle of complementarity for psychology. *American Psychologist, 48*, 933–942.

Salovey, P. 1990. Interview. *American Scientist*, January, February, 25–29.

Schuller, Robert H. 1982. *Self-esteem: the new reformation*. Waco, TX: Word Books.

Schultz, Duane, and Schultz, Sydney E. 1996. *A history of modern psychology*. (6th ed.). New York: Harcourt Brace College Publishers.

Sechenov, I.M. 1863. *Reflexes of the brain* (S. Belsky, trans.). Cambridge, Mass.: M.I.T. Press, 1965.

Seligman, M.E.P. 1975. *Helplessness: on depression, development and death*. San Francisco: Freeman.

Seligman, M.E.P. 1991. *Learned optimism*. New York: Knopf.

Smith, Adam. 1776. *An inquiry into the nature and causes of the wealth of nations*.

Smith, Ronald E. 1993. *Psychology*. New York: West Publishing Co.

Spence, Kenneth W. 1956. *Behavior theory and conditioning*. New Haven: Yale University Press.

Sperry, Roger. 1985. Changed concepts of brain and consciousness: some value implications. *Zygon, 20*, 41–57.

Sperry, Roger. 1993. The impact and promise of the cognitive revolution. *American Psychologist, 48*, 878–885.

Strupp, Hans H., and Howard, Kenneth. 1992. A brief history of psychotherapy research. In Freeheim, Donald K. (Ed.). *History of psychotherapy: a century of change*. Washington, DC: American Psychological Association.

Szasz, Thomas S. 1970. *Ideology and insanity*. Garden City, NY: Doubleday and Company.

Taylor, S.E. 1989. *Positive illusions*. New York: Basic Books.

Tillich, Paul. 1948. *The shaking of the foundations*. New York: C. Scribner's Sons.

Tillich, Paul. 1963. *Systematic theology* (Vol. III). Chicago: University of Chicago Press.

Tillich, Paul. 1967. *My search for absolutes*. New York: Simon and Schuster.

Titus, Harold. 1953. *Living issues in philosophy*. New York: American Book Company.

Ulanov, Ann, and Ulanov, Barry. 1975. *Religion and the unconscious*. Philadelphia: The Westminster Press.

Vandenbos, Gary R., Nicholas A. Cummings, and Patrick H. DeLeon. 1992. A century of psychotherapy: economic and environmental influences. In Friedheim, Donald K. (Ed.). *History of psychotherapy: a century of change*. Washington, DC: American Psychological Association.

Vitz, Paul. 1977. *Psychology as religion: the cult of self-worship*. Grand Rapids, MI: Eerdmans.

Watson, J.B. 1914. *Behavior: an introduction to comparative psychology*. New York: Holt.

Weber, Max. 1930. *The Protestant ethic and the spirit of capitalism*. (trans by Talcott Parsons, with a foreword by R. H. Tawney.). New York: Scribner.

Wolterstorff, Nicholas. 1976. *Reason within the bounds of religion*. (2nd ed.). Grand Rapids, MI: Eerdmans.

Index